MAKE YOUR ILLNESS COUNT

Vernon J. Bittner

AUGSBURG PUBLISHING HOUSE
MINNEAPOLIS, MINNESOTA

MAKE YOUR ILLNESS COUNT

Copyright © 1976 Augsburg Publishing House

Library of Congress Catalog Card No. 76-3862

International Standard Book No. 0-8066-1532-X

Scripture quotations unless otherwise noted are from the Revised Standard Version of the Bible, copyright 1946, 1952, and 1971 by the Division of Christian Education of the National Council of Churches.

MANUFACTURED IN THE UNITED STATES OF AMERICA

Contents

About the Author

Dr. Vernon J. Bittner is internationally recognized as a leader in Clinical Pastoral Education. He earned his doctorate in psychology and religion. He served as a parish pastor in Minneapolis for ten years.

He was the first in the United States to establish a fully accredited Clinical Pastoral Education program in a parish setting. He organized the only hospital-based police chaplaincy corps in the United States. This chaplaincy corps serves 14 metropolitan communities.

In addition to teaching Clinical Pastoral Education in this country, he has taught counseling and methods of group therapy at a neuro-psychiatric hospital in West Germany. He has been a lecturer at several seminaries and a contributor to many journals.

Chaplain Bittner is accredited by the American Association of Marriage and Family Counselors, the American Association of Pastoral Counselors, the Association for Clinical Pastoral Education, Inc., and the American Protestant Hospital Association.

To

those who have accepted
the opportunities of illness.

Acknowledgments

When I think of all the people who have encouraged me I am aware that there are almost enough to fill this book.

Of all of these, the individuals and families who have helped me most are those who have allowed me to share in their illnesses. By opening themselves up to me, they allowed me to be exposed not only to the human predicament of illness, but also to the opportunity for health and happiness.

I wish to pay tribute to my colleagues with whom I have shared many learning experiences, to the administration and staff of North Memorial Medical Center who have supported me, to numerous physicians who have encouraged me, and to my secretary Mrs. Joyce Knutsen.

I also want to thank my family and those who have made me a part of their family for sharing in my journey to this point.

I especially want to thank my Lord, who makes everything of value happen—past, present, and future.

had become dormant, with people whose faith was different from mine, or with agnostics. Perhaps less than 40 percent of the hospital patients had any kind of significant belief.

This made the experience of illness even more significant and my ministry in the hospital more demanding. I know how difficult it is to use illness constructively, whether a person believes in God or not. I also know that the experience of illness often becomes the opportunity many people need to stop running long enough to find a happier, more fruitful life. Sometimes a person does have to get sick to get better, at least emotionally and spiritually, if not physically.

The more I am with people who are sick, the more I realize how difficult it is to face illness. I believe I can help those who suffer. This ability to help is not only from what I have read, though that often helps. Nor is it limited to what I have learned from the experiences of others, though patients have taught me a great deal. I have learned most from the experience of having to face the realities of life myself. I have had to go through my dark valley. During that time I was lifted and comforted by the strength of those close to me. Their own experiences made them good listeners. They were able to confront me with reality and to help me see that I could do something positive with my illness if I chose to do so.

My illness was the vehicle through which I became more real and alive to life. My illness taught me to see more fully the love and forgiveness of God. God did love me. He not only loved me in spite of myself, but because of myself. Illness was the opportunity I needed to change from a path of self-destruction to a new life of being alive to God, to others, and to myself.

In this book I want to tell about healing in the lives of those I have served, and to share the healing that has occurred in my own life. Illness, like nothing else, makes us aware of our own limitations. This can encourage us to be more open to ourselves, others, and God, or it can result in our being more closed as individuals. How we use this experience is up to us. Unfortunately, too many people look at illness as a waste of time or as something to be avoided. They do not see it as an opportunity for maturity, wisdom, and service. Such patients do not make their illness count.

I pray that you who are ill or who have loved ones who are ill will benefit from my experience and the experiences of those I have met. I pray that God may use this book to strengthen your faith so that you may see more fully the constructive use of your illness.

With God's help you can make your illness count.

Prayer of a New Patient

Dear Lord,
It's morning and here is that light and sound
    all over again . . .
Except that it is unfamiliar.
It's not the friendly sound of home.
Doctors are being paged,
    and carts are passing by the door.
I'm feeling isolated and all alone,
    and I'm feeling a little scared because
    I don't know what today will bring.
Help me to know that you are with me.
Lord, guide the minds and the hands of the doctors,
    nurses, therapists, technicians—
    all who seek to heal.
And Lord, take hold of me so I may cooperate with
    you.
And guide those who are concerned about my health,
    that healing might occur physically,
    emotionally, and spiritually.

                                    Amen

1

DOES GOD
WANT ME TO BE ILL?

I cry aloud to God;
   I cry aloud, and he hears me.
In time of trouble I pray to the Lord;
   all night long I lift my hands in prayer,
   but I cannot find comfort.
I think of God, and I sigh;
   I meditate, and I feel discouraged.

"Will the Lord always reject me?
   Will he never again be pleased with me?
Has he stopped loving me?
   Is his promise no longer good?
Has God forgotten to be merciful?
   Has anger taken the place of his compassion?

I will remember your great acts, Lord;
   I will recall the wonders you did in the past.
I will think about all that you have done;
   I will meditate on all your deeds.

By your power you saved your people,
   the descendants of Jacob and of Joseph.

PSALM 77 (TEV)

Every morning when I walk into North Memorial Medical Center I sense that a drama is being played out in the lives of many people. As I walk through Admitting and the Department of Trauma and Acute

Medicine, I am aware that these people have suddenly moved from that which is familiar, routine, and comfortable into a world of illness, doubt, and anxiety. Undeniably, it is dramatic.

It is also traumatic. Behind every tear, every worry, and every sigh of hope there is someone in the hospital for whom the world has closed in. Instead of the crisis happening to someone else, it has now occurred to "me."

Sometimes I wish I had the ability to write music to express what I feel and experience. In my fantasy I wonder if music would be a better way to express the breadth of the life-death events that I see taking place. The suffering, hope, despair, and joy are all there. But there is triumph, too. Not always the triumph of physical recovery, but the triumph of emotional and spiritual recovery. It is a triumph that occurs when illness causes a person to find a more meaningful life.

What Is Illness?

Dictionaries define illness this way: "a state of being in poor health," or "a sickness or disease." For our purposes, however, this definition is rather shallow. Illness includes much more. *Illness is the expression of our own physical, emotional, or spiritual limitations.* When you accept illness you really accept that you are human, and that as a human you have limitations. One of those limitations is that you can become ill. Because our culture is quite successful in avoiding this fact illness for many of us is difficult to tolerate or to accept.

I want to make it very clear that having difficulty facing illness does not mean that you do not have enough faith or that your illness is the result of not having a personal experience with God. This is not the way it is. Almost everyone has had, and will have, difficulty facing illness.

The problem of accepting illness, however, is not so much that of accepting physical pain or the length of time you have been sick; how disabling or disfiguring it may be, or how emotionally drained you may be. The problem is rather the absence of meaning in this experience.

In the Old Testament, Job was tormented not so much by his pain as he was by the question, "Why did this happen to me?" Nietzsche put it this way: The problem is not suffering in itself, but rather that the answer to the question, "Why suffer?" is missing. If illness is a waste of time, as many think, some meaning must be found in illness, so that it is more than just a waste of time.

There is a problem, however, with this idea because in our age personal value is assessed by our ability to produce. When we cease to be productive, society places minimal value upon us. When we are ill we need the desire to retain our value even if we are no longer able to work. We need to learn that life has a deeper meaning than merely working from 8:00 to 5:00. Society honors the successful person and measures human values on the basis of a person's success or failure. Success and honor do not alone determine a person's worth. Illness has worth, too, in the meaning of life. Illness can mean the opportunity for fulfillment *if you are willing to accept that there is meaning in illness.* Many people are willing and can find meaning in illness, but for others unfortunately it seems impossible.

The Story of Joe

The voice on the other end of the phone was from the Intensive Care Unit. They were having trouble with a man who had just come in with a heart attack. He was restless and refusing treatment.

As I came to the door of his room I could hear Joe telling the nurse that she knew where the door was and she knew what to do with her needles.

I introduced myself and said, "It sounds like you're having a bad time."

"I sure am. It's bad enough to be *here*. They won't give you any peace. If they're not taking blood, they're taking your pulse. And if they're not pushing pills they want to give you a shot."

"You have the feeling they don't understand what you're going through."

"That's right! All they want to do is make you miserable!"

"What do you think is making you feel the *most* miserable right now?" I said.

"What do you mean?"

"It seems to me that the greatest discomfort you are having right now is the result of your anger. If you don't calm down they will have to give you another shot. Otherwise you may have another heart attack and I know you don't want that."

Joe thought for a moment. He began to tap his fingers on the bed stand. He didn't like what I said.

Finally he said, "I don't want another heart attack, that's for sure. I just want to get well and get out of the hospital."

I told him this would only be possible if he were willing to cooperate. Momentarily he began to calm down. I decided to leave. I told him I would see him again. He thanked me and told me he would like me to come back.

I saw Joe regularly for short periods of time. After five days he left that unit and went to another unit to convalesce for several weeks. There he continued to give the nurses a bad time. I tried to help him see that he needed to do something about his anger. Not only did his anger make it difficult for the nursing staff, but it also made it impossible for him to regain and maintain his health. But he continued to talk at length about his anger at God.

Didn't God know that he was the top executive of his firm? Did God want him to be sick? And why, anyway, does God allow illness? Certainly God knew there would be illness, and if he knew, why didn't he do something about it?

I tried to explain that it was normal to be angry, but that God didn't want him to be sick even though he had allowed it to happen. God's will for him was that he have life, joy, and health. Unfortunately, when humans rebelled against God, evil came into the world, and along with it sickness, pain, and death.

I told him that God loved him and all people in spite of our rebellion against him. However, the result of our rebellion was illness instead of health, pain instead of joy, and death instead of life. *But* God still gave us the power through his Son to have health, joy, and life, if not completely in this world, then in the life to come.

Nothing I said helped Joe. He continued to be angry toward God. His activity had been stopped and all he could think about was getting back to work. Being sick was a waste of time. Work was his whole life. Before his heart attack he worked endless hours. He was highly respected and he had gained considerable social prestige. In spite of his apparent impatience, he was able to be considerate of his subordinates with a veneer of warmth.

He was a family man. His son and daughter were in their early twenties. His devoted wife, Diane, had always supported him, even in his pride of being a self-made man.

Prior to his coronary some problems had greatly upset him. Some of his management personnel had neglected their responsibilities. He was aware of this, but he was unwilling to face the situation. If he did, it would be a reflection on him, he thought. People would see that he was not the perfect executive. He thought he needed to maintain this image to remain the perfect administrator in his own eyes. He had no room for being upset, anxious, or depressed. There was no time at work or at home to talk about his difficulties. Self-made men don't need anyone else. At least, this is what he told himself. If he were to admit to these problems he would place himself in the position of not being the perfect executive. He was too insecure for that.

His wife Diane found her life purpose in supporting him in his game. She, too, liked being the wife of a "very important person." Her identity was dependent on his being the perfect executive. If she were to see him unable to solve his own problems, her confidence would be shaken. Yet Diane resented his need to run everything. At times she would even indicate to him and to others how dissatisfied she was in having to keep "her mouth shut" and "play the fool," just to reinforce him in his superficial role.

But the stress for Joe was too great. Because of his need for success, his need to be in charge, his need to solve everything himself, and his unwillingness to change, he had a heart attack. His value system made it very difficult for him to feel anything but anger and frustration over his situation. In some way he needed to redefine his values and understand his true value as a child of God. I tried to help him see that we are all God's children and that God does not want us to be ill in spite of the fact that he allows illness to happen. Unfortunately, he was unable to accept this. Two months later he was brought in by ambulance, dead on arrival. His unwillingness to accept his human limitations and the unresolved anger had killed him. Because he was unwilling to change his value system he placed himself in a "no-win" situation and he died of a coronary.

Just as some are unwilling to accept their illness because they are overcome by anger, there are those who resent being sick but are willing to resolve their anger so that their illness can be a meaningful experience. The following is an example.

It's Cancer

Cary was eighteen, the high school homecoming queen, active in her church, and an excellent student. It was the spring of her senior year. She was brought in with severe abdominal pain. Exploratory surgery was scheduled. Her surgery was quick. The cancer was inoperable. It was throughout her abdomen.

I was called by 6 North to go to see her. Cary was a lovely girl. Not only was she beautiful to look at, but as I discovered later, she had an even greater inner beauty.

The cancer patient has to bear many stresses and burdens. It takes a special effort to deal adequately with the resentment that accompanies this illness.

Cary was constantly bothered by nausea that compounded the pain. This continued after the surgery because it accomplished nothing more than to let the doctors know they could do nothing except give her chemotherapy and keep her as comfortable as possible.

After a short time she became strong enough to go home. She was not able to attend classes but she was able to finish her school work at home so she could be graduated.

As the weeks passed she experienced one of the other stresses of cancer, disfigurement. Because she was continuing to lose weight and her tumor continued to grow, Cary took on the appearance of being pregnant.

This was an embarrassment to her. I recall how resentful this made her feel. This bothered her so much that she didn't want to see anyone. Even her friends, and she had many of them, had the feeling that they were not wanted.

The disfigurement caused her to be more concerned about the future. As her tumor continued to grow, she became more frail and weak. She was forced to face the thought of her own death. As a Christian it was hard for her to reconcile a God of love with a God who would allow this.

The more she thought about this the more resentful she became. One day as I was talking with her about this, she lashed out at God and shrieked, "I hate you, God. I hate you!"

As her illness progressed she was oppressed by the thought that her life seemed to have no purpose. She would have no chance to pursue a vocation, to be a wife, or to be a mother. All of these things she would be denied.

Her life seemed meaningless. She found herself becoming dependent on others, even to the point of needing help in dressing herself. It was bad enough to have nothing to look forward to in the future. Now she had even lost the meaning in life that comes from being able to take care of one's self.

For her, life seemed empty and she felt as though she was of no value because she couldn't even dress herself. She began to feel that she was not worth caring about.

Cary, like most of us, had grown up with the idea that her value as a person is only in the ability to produce and to take care of one's self. Fortunately, God has never said that. Rather, God tells us that our value is in our belonging to him. We are his children. All of us need to believe that. One day we will all come to the time when we will be unable to care for ourselves and will have to give up our occupation. Even then we can still find meaning in the love God has for us. He loves us for who we are and not for what we can do.

Cary was not able to accept this at first. Instead, she began to insulate herself from what people were saying to her and isolate herself from those who loved her and wanted to care for her. She built a wall around herself. She was on the inside and those who wanted to care for her were on the outside. And in her aloneness she became filled with self-pity. This was the result of her unwillingness to do anything about her anger. *Self-pity is one of the results of unresolved anger.*

Her disease seemed to progress more rapidly as her attitude deteriorated. She no longer forced herself to eat or drink. She became dehydrated. Her doctors recommended that she come back into the hospital.

I saw Cary on the second day of her hospitalization. She was very weak and withdrawn. I asked her if there were anything she would like to talk about. I waited for what seemed like ten minutes. There was no response. Even her physical appearance was saying she wanted to be alone, because she kept staring off into space.

Then I told her that I would like to say something to her, if that was all right. She consented reluctantly. I told her that many people were concerned about her. I told her I was concerned, too, but that her attitude of not letting anyone care for her was frustrating to all of us.

"Yeah," she said, "I'll bet they care! Who could care about me? Look at me! I can't even take care of myself—and I look ugly!"

She began to cry. I took her hand. For a few moments I said nothing. I just listened to her cry. She needed to cry. She needed to get the hurt out. For a long time she had been carrying it all by herself. She had isolated herself. She was finally letting the wall down.

"I have the feeling," I said, "that you're very angry at God for allowing this to happen. And I feel that you're really very angry at yourself for feeling that way."

"Yes, I am. And I have been for some time. I know that he doesn't want me to be sick and that he doesn't cause illness, but—well, it's so hard to accept."

"I'm sure it is," I said. "But what do you think is making it even harder?"

"What do you mean?"

"I mean," I said, "that you are making it more difficult because of your attitude. The very thing you need right now is to allow those around you to love you. But because you are so resentful about your illness you have isolated yourself from us. Will you let us love you?"

She began to cry again. Then, shaking her head affirmingly, she said softly, "Yes."

I asked Cary what she thought she would have to do to let those around her love her. She realized that she would have to do something about her anger. Her anger was keeping the wall up, causing her to isolate herself from those she loved and those who loved her and resulting in her feeling sorry for herself.

I asked her if I could help with her anger. She said, "Yes, I'd like to get rid of it."

"How can you get rid of it?" I asked.

Without any hesitation she said, "I'll have to forgive God!"

"Would you like to do that?"

"Yes!"

"Why don't you tell God that you do forgive him?" I said. "Do you want to do that right now?"

I could see that this was hard for her. It wasn't easy to give up her anger. Now she would have to do something about changing her attitude toward her illness, especially her self-pity. Besides, she would have to stop isolating herself from people. She would have to let people love her and also respond to their love. This would be painful because she would have to give them up again, because she knew she didn't have long to live. Yet she needed to love and be loved. Without it life holds little good for any of us.

Once she had forgiven God she was able to forgive herself as well. The wall she had built with resentment, isolation, and self-pity came down. Even though she knew she had cancer and that she would die very soon, she had now made it possible for others to share her experience with her. Death is the one experience we must endure by ourselves, because no one can die with us. Cary knew that, but she would know the comfort, strength, and hope that is found in sharing in the experience of dying with

those who love her and a God who would never
forsake her in life or in death.

Forgiveness: The Solution for Anger

About a week later I received a call to go to Cary's
room. She had requested her family to come to the
hospital to hear what she wanted to tell them.

She had asked me to be there, too. She felt that
her family would need me. Besides, she wanted me
to hear what she had to say.

It was still winter. Almost a year had passed since
her first hospitalization. Everyone seemed to sense
that today would be the end.

The family was gathered around her bed. It was
difficult for her to talk but she needed to tell them
what was on her mind.

"I know now that God loves me and that's all I
need to know. For a long time during my illness I
was angry at God because I thought he had caused
this to happen to me. Now I know that he did not
cause it to happen, but he did allow me to become
ill. Please forgive me for making it so difficult for
you to love me. Thank you all for continuing to love
me even though I acted so unlovable at times.

"There is one more thing I want to say. Don't be
sad about my death, because I'm looking forward
to it, because God will be with me. I love you all.
I'm very tired now and I want to rest."

She closed her eyes and fell asleep. She never
regained consciousness. Death came a day later.
During that day there was no evidence of any pain
or discomfort.

She had accepted her death; in fact, she was looking forward to it. There was beauty in the observance of her dying. She had forgiven God so that it was possible for her to accept her illness and her dying. She had experienced comfort, strength, and hope from her family and from God. God and her family had shared in her death with her.

But more important, because of her illness, life had taken on an added dimension. Cary and her family had experienced more fully than ever before the joy of loving and being loved by one another and by God. Through her illness, Cary had found what some people never find.

In your illness you may find that you have had all the feelings of this patient. You may also find that these feelings come and go as your illness progresses or as you feel isolated from God and the important others in your life. In the following chapters I will deal with each of these feelings in depth. I hope to show you how to cope with your feelings so they won't become destructive to you and others. I will do this by helping you to use your emotional and spiritual resources. I hope to show how you can use your emotional and spiritual strength to find meaning in your illness.

Unfortunately, most of us don't discard the destructive things in life until we are forced to do it, either by a crisis or some other outside force. You may have to get sick before you can get better. Sometimes the only way people grow in maturity, wisdom, and service to others is to find a way to make their illness count.

Lord, I've been angry and resentful.
Being sick is hard to accept:
    the discomfort from the pain and nausea;
    the embarrassment of looking like I'm pregnant;
    the frustration of having future dreams shattered;
    the meaninglessness of being dependent;
    the hopelessness of being isolated from those I love
      and
    the helplessness of feeling immobilized by my own
      self-pity.

Lord, at times being sick in body, mind, and spirit seems
      overwhelming.
That wall that I have created seems so necessary, and so
      safe.
But I've isolated myself, and I've insulated myself as well.
I am alone, Lord.
I don't even have You!

But there is forgiveness.
Thank you, Lord, for that.

It is only in forgiving
    that resentment is replaced by love,
    that loneliness is replaced by belonging, and
    that self-pity is replaced by hope.
It is only in forgiving that I am forgiven.

                                Amen

2

TELL ME
IT'S NOT SERIOUS

*Now the Lord is the Spirit; where the Spirit of the
Lord is, there is freedom.*   2 CORINTHIANS 3:17

As a young boy, I grew up with the idea that
children are supposed to be happy. I recall the
nursery rhymes and the short stories for children
that ended, ". . . and they lived happily ever after."
This fantasy was shattered very quickly, because
when I was seven my mother died of cancer. I
was forced to face the unpleasant reality that not
all things end happily.

I remember that experience well. We were living
in a small southwestern Minnesota town. In those
days our town had no mortuary. There was a morti-
cian, but not a mortuary.

The custom was to keep the body in the home.
This made it difficult to deny the reality of death.
I remember how "spooky" it was to have the dead
body of my mother in the house. We moved some
of the furniture out of the living room to make room

33

for the casket. People came to our house for the reviewal.

I knew her body was there, but a part of me wanted to deny her death. I needed her. I wanted her to be alive.

On the day of the funeral I got up very early while everyone else was still sleeping. I remember how strange I felt being in the same room with her. I felt like running. I didn't even want to stay in the house, so I left. My father had to come to find me. He was angry. Didn't I know that the funeral was today and many things had to be done? He told me that I was making things more difficult. The least I could do was to stay at home so he wouldn't have to look for me.

I felt bad. I knew what he was saying was true. I just didn't like it in the house. But I told him I wouldn't leave again.

The service concluded with the family viewing the body. After they had paid their last respects, the congregation did the same. This was a terrible ordeal for me. I recall how self-conscious I was about walking up in front of all those people. I was walking with my father. He kept pushing me to go ahead of him. I walked up, looked at my mother, and started to walk away.

Suddenly someone grabbed my arm. I found myself being pulled back toward the casket. What was this for? I had seen her. I had been with her dead body for almost two days. Wasn't that enough? My father let me know that I wasn't acting appropriately, at least according to him. The proper thing to do was to spend some time in front of the casket. I know now that in his grief it was hard for him to leave her and say good-bye. He wanted me to be with him. He was having difficulty accepting his overwhelming feelings of loss.

My memory of the rest of that day is rather vague. I don't remember the cemetery, and I don't recall the "fellowship hour" afterwards. But as I reflect on this experience, I am aware that I was trying to deny the fact that my mother was dead. Even though her body was in our house I did not want to accept her death. I wanted to run away from it.

Most of us are like this. We don't want to accept the truth that life is sometimes unhappy. However, as time went on this experience helped me to enter the real world. I began to realize that I should be grateful for whatever happiness I was able to find. This experience, even though traumatic, had helped me to grow up. It had taught me that denying unpleasant things doesn't make them go away. But I had more growing up to do.

It is difficult to accept that life is not always happy. We live wiith the great American dream that this is the land of happiness. As a result, we expect happiness. Consequently, disappointment and illness are hard to accept. So whenever illness comes it seems to be incomprehensible. We absorb a philosophy that says, "If you go to church, serve God, and love your neighbor, you'll be happy and free from illness."

Thomas Jefferson defined happiness as "not being pained in body or troubled in mind." Therefore, if happiness was the result of living the "good" life one could assume that illness in any form would not occur. With that mind-set, happiness had no responsibility attached to it. Being happy meant being without physical, emotional, or spiritual pain.

If you grow up with a philosophy of life that makes avoiding pain your goal, it's no wonder that denial is a prominent part of life. In our historical past our forefathers were pioneers who endured hardships, but we have become almost allergic to illness and suffering. Whenever illness comes, we not only want to avoid its seriousness, but we want to avoid being sick altogether. No one likes to hear that life's pleasant routine is being interrupted or to look at the oppressing idea that as human beings we have limitations.

We would generally rather dream and "fantasize" about a savior—either God, a doctor, an exorcist, a guru, or a pastor—who will make it all better. The desire is strong for someone else to assume responsibility for our illness and our attitude toward it. Most of us want to deny its existence.

The following is an illustration of a woman who used her period of illness as a time to deny its reality. This resulted in continued illness, feeling miserable emotionally and spiritually, and finding no positive value in her illness.

A Family Request

A family came into my office to tell me about their mother, Faye, who wasn't getting well. There was really no reason for this. Her surgery, though major, was a routine operation. Several months previous Faye had undergone a hysterectomy, apparently successful. She returned home with the idea that she would have to remain inactive for a while and that she would need two to three months to recuperate.

A short time after her return home she began to hemorrhage and was rushed back to the hospital. Faye improved but every time she seemed well enough to go home she would develop complications. Finally she was transferred to our hospital for further tests.

As I entered the room I saw a frail, limp, middle-aged woman. Her hair was partially gray. Her face was drawn. Her eyes seemed sad and a tear was running down her cheek.

I introduced myself and informed her that her family had asked me to see her. Faye told me she knew that and said she was glad I had come.

"You're having a bad time with your illness!"

"I sure am. It's really discouraging. It's one thing after another. Now I've got phlebitis. I've just got to get home—my family needs me. But I guess they are getting along. . . . I just had a pain pill so I feel a little groggy. You might know they'd give me one, now—now that my family has left. What's worse is that I am not even able to sleep. I know I've got to sleep to get well, but as soon as it gets quiet I'm awake."

As she continued to talk about her situation I became more and more convinced that this woman was not getting well because she was unable to accept her illness. Apparently she had gone home from the hospital after her surgery and had begun to work as though she had never undergone major surgery.

Unfortunately, this woman was not able to see any value in her illness. She was able to see value only in taking care of her family. She was unable to realize that as a child of God she was of value whether or not she could perform as a wife and a mother.

Duties and responsible work do give meaning to life, but a meaningful life is not dependent on doing. In fact, some people are so busy *doing* that they aren't *being* persons. They pass up the opportunity to *be* the persons God created them to be, because they are so busy running from one thing to another. They have not learned that their primary value comes from being children of God. Their value is in who they are.

This woman denied her value as a person. As a result she became more ill physically because she was denying her illness as well. Illness, for Faye, was something to be avoided and she was doing everything she could to pretend that it didn't exist. The more she avoided it, the more apparent her illness became. She was not getting well. Instead of using her emotional and spiritual resources to face reality she was using them to deny reality. Her resources were not helping her to get well but were causing her to develop one complication after another. Because she was unwilling to accept her illness she was making herself more ill.

How do you accept illness? How can you use your religious and emotional resources to avoid denial and avoid becoming more ill? How are you able to accept being sick so it's not just a waste of time?

The following situation is an example of an individual who used his emotional and spiritual resources to accept his illness at long last and to help others accept theirs.

Denial Overcome by Hope

Almost every day our office is called by the hospital staff to see certain patients. This day was no exception. One of the referrals was from 5 West. A patient was going to have an ileostomy and wanted to see a chaplain before his surgery. (An ileostomy is a surgical creation of an opening into the ileum, or small intestine, by establishing a minute opening on the abdominal wall.)

Bob was a handsome young man in his early twenties. He had a pleasant look on his face. I had the feeling that he was struggling not to show anyone that he was very concerned about his surgery. Nonverbally, he was saying this to me by the rigid way in which he was lying on his bed.

"I know my condition is serious," he said. "I have been bothered by colitis for some time, but I haven't let it get me down."

I could tell, though, that it was getting him down. He was flat on his back and about to have surgery, but I didn't think that challenging him before surgery was appropriate. I knew I would upset him if I did and I knew there wasn't time enough to help him get that resolved before he went to surgery.

In spite of my uneasiness regarding the denial of his feelings, I was willing to allow him to gloss over his emotional discomfort. Later I found out that this seemed to be the pattern of his life. He not only denied his anxieties about his illness, but about many

other things as well. All of his life he had resented
his mother. These feelings had been repressed so
long, however, that he was not even aware that he
had them. In fact, he wasn't aware of feeling much
of anything. Yet every time his mother disappointed
him, his resentment was being expressed somatically.
By denying his resentment he unknowingly was
destroying his small intestine. Denying his resentment had caused his body to produce more hydro-
chloric acid than was necessary for digestion. It had
perforated his small intestine. Surgery was the only
recourse.

I tried to help him spiritually by reassuring him
that God was with him and that I was sure he would
guide the hands of the surgeon so that this operation
would be a success. I told him as I left that I would
be back to see him after surgery. He told me that
he would appreciate another visit. The surgery was
successful.

On the third day after surgery I went back to see
him. Even though he still had some discomfort he
was feeling much better, but he seemed depressed.
He was having difficulty accepting his ileostomy.
I had worked with patients like this before and I
knew it wasn't an easy thing to accept. He was telling
me by his depressed attitude that he really wasn't
accepting the situation.

"You seem depressed today," I said.

"Yes," he said, "but this thing isn't going to get me
down. I'll be just as good as new."

I asked him what he meant by that.

"I have had all kinds of difficulties in my life and
they didn't get me down either."

Then he told me about his alcoholic mother. She had been divorced from his father when Bob was a young boy, and as the oldest child he had become the responsible one in the family. Not only had he "parented" his five young brothers and sisters, but his mother as well. Without him the family couldn't have managed.

"What will the other children do? Who will take care of them? I can't be sick!" he said.

"But you are sick," I said. "And denying it will make you more ill. Your need for an ileostomy is not only evidence that you have made yourself more ill, but it is also the result of not accepting your illness."

I wanted him to see that it was impossible to do everything, that even *he* had limitations. He could not assume responsibility for the children and his mother as well as for himself. He could be responsible only for himself. Furthermore, he was of value whether he took care of the children and his mother or not. In fact, his refusal to take care of himself was really his way of denying that he was sick.

"You must accept that you are sick in order to get well," I said.

"But I can't," he said. "I don't want to die! I can't die. They need me. What will they do without me? My mother can't take care of them!"

He was denying his illness because he had convinced himself that if he accepted his illness he was going to die.

Does anyone want to accept his illness if it means death? This was not only Bob's problem, but the problem of many people who are ill. They deny their illness because they do not want to accept the possibility that their illness may result in death.

Bob was convinced that accepting his illness meant "giving up." It meant giving up the kind of life that was destroying him, but it did not mean to give up living. He would have to give in to the idea that he was a human being, with certain limitations.

Unfortunately, when he left the hospital he was again determined to be in control of himself and his situation. I did not hear from him for some time until I received a call from his mother. She told me he did not seem to be getting any better. He had gone back to work for a while, but had become so weak that he spent the last two weeks at home.

I recommended that she get him to their family physician without delay. Within five hours he was back in the hospital.

Between his first hospital stay and this one I had been thinking about him. I had wondered why his illness was so threatening, beyond the fact that no one wants to be ill. I was convinced that for him giving up meant losing control, and losing control meant that he might have to talk about some of the things he didn't want to talk about.

After a few days he felt better and began to regain his strength. When I stopped by to see him again he was his usual cheerful self—at least on the surface. But his body was telling me how rigid and tense he felt.

I told him that I had been thinking about him. I tried to convey to him how concerned I was, especially now that he had come back to the hospital again.

"There is something I would like to say to you," I said, "but I don't know if I should or not."

"Go ahead; it's okay."

"I think I know now why you have continued to deny your illness," I said. "If you accept your illness you may also have to accept some negative feelings that you have never looked at regarding your mother."

There was a long silence. His body became restless and fidgety. I could see that thinking about this was bothering him. He began to speak. At first, haltingly. Soon it began to flow out of him. He talked at length about how he had been hurt by his mother's drinking, how she had mistreated them, and how this had resulted in his father leaving. I tried to help him to see that when we are hurt by people we love, the feeling we have is resentment. Unfortunately, because he had repressed his feelings for so long he did not even know he was resentful. Instead of telling his mother how she had hurt him, he held his feelings inside. He had learned that to express them only made her more upset. He was living the philosophy of "peace at any price," the price of destroying himself.

As we talked about it, he became aware that he was resentful and angry, that it was normal to be angry at a parent who had hurt him as much as his mother had. But the denial of this resentment and hurt was making him sick. I told him that I would be willing to help him, if he wanted help. He wanted help, he said, but he had difficulty believing there could be any help for him or for his mother.

I asked him if he believed in God and if he believed me when I told him that there was an alternative for him and his mother. I asked him if he would give God and me a chance to help him. He said he would. I explained that he would have to stop denying his illness and his negative feelings. He would have to risk trusting God and me. He would have to be willing to believe there was hope for his situation. If he would be willing to hope, he might be surprised how bold he could become. God could help him face his illness, resolve his negative feelings, and even give him the strength to stop allowing his mother to deny her illness of alcoholism.

During his hospitalization he began to realize that to hope in God was the answer for his life. Previously, he had believed that there was no hope. This is why he had to cover up his illness, his hurt feelings, and his mother's illness. He had believed that only he could solve the problems at home, and if he accepted his illness and his negative feelings he would not be able to handle the situation at home. He would collapse.

Now he realized that the only solution was to rely on God's help to solve his dilemma. He could not do it alone.

I knew he would have to forgive his mother, because his unresolved resentment toward her was making him sick. This was hard. She had hurt him deeply. He realized that she was sick and that her illness was the reason why she had not loved him the way he deserved to be loved.

After he had struggled for several days and realized how his anger was hurting him he became reconciled with his mother and began to feel better physically and spiritually. He gained confidence. His hope had helped him. Now he would have to try to help his mother. This would be very difficult. It is always hard for a child to tell a parent to get some help. I told him I would be willing to help.

We decided the best plan would be to ask her to meet with the two of us. It would be easier for her to accept it from me than from him. I suggested he tell her that I needed to talk to her in order to help him. This would be much less threatening to her. If he told her that she needed help she might not come at all.

This seemed the best approach because his health was somewhat dependent on her getting help for herself. If she continued to abuse him and the children, he might revert back to his old patterns.

She agreed to come in and I saw her alone for a few minutes. I wanted her to understand how she was a part of Bob's problem. She was very defensive and at first denied that she had anything to do with her son's problem. I asked her if she thought she might have a drinking problem. I wanted her to see that people who have problems when they drink usually have a drinking problem.

She grasped the arms of the chair as if she had to keep herself from drowning. My question was difficult for her to face, but deep within she knew she had a problem. She confessed that for some time she had suspected it but she didn't want to believe it. She didn't want to accept it because she had become dependent on it. She needed it, she thought. Alcohol had given her the freedom to express her anger, frustration, and feeling of failure regarding her own life. Unfortunately, under the influence of alcohol, her feelings were being expressed in an inappropriate way.

I asked her if she wanted to change. She told me she wanted to quit. She tried to convince herself and me that she could do it alone, but she had known about her problem for years and she hadn't done anything about it. Why would it be any different now?

There was a long pause. A war was going on inside. This was evident again by the way she kept hanging on to the chair. I asked her if she wanted to tell her son what we had talked about. Hesitantly, she agreed.

She told him she had a drinking problem and that she was going to quit. Bob told her how happy this made him feel. But he indicated to her that he believed she needed to go into an alcoholic treatment center. He didn't think she could conquer her problem alone.

I was surprised to hear him say that. He had never told his mother what he thought before. And somehow his mother knew that she would not be able to change his mind. He wouldn't back down this time. He had found the courage he needed. He had given in to God and had found strength beyond himself. God had given him boldness and power that he had never experienced before.

Through the hope that he had found in God he was not only able to avoid the denial of his own illness and the cause of it (denial of his hurt feelings), but he also helped his mother stop denying her problem. Through hope in God, Bob had removed the veil of denial. He had experienced freedom that only the Lord can give. He had experienced the significance of hope in his life.

Bob made his illness count. His illness became the most meaningful experience in his life.

Lord, I'm sick . . .
And I don't want to be sick.
I have things to do,
Places to go,
People to meet.
I don't have time to be sick.

Lord, do you hear me!
I said, I don't want to be sick!
But I am sick, Lord . . . and it's painful.
Painful because I've always been so active,
Always had it my way,
Always been in control,
And now I am out of control.

Lord, help me!
Help me to feel okay even though I'm out of control.
Help me to feel okay even though I'm not doing well.
Lord, help me to stop running, avoiding, so
I can start living.

Lord, give me some hope!
Help me to see illness as life.
Help me to see death as life.
Lord, help me to be truly alive, again,
By accepting my illness.

Amen

3

WHY ME?

If we confess our sins, he is faithful and just, and will forgive our sins and cleanse us from all unrighteousness.   1 JOHN 1:9

In the last year of my seminary education I made the amazing discovery that my feeling of guilt had a strong influence in my decision to become a pastor. This realization came to me during my first quarter of Clinical Pastoral Education, a training program for clergy in pastoral counseling and group dynamics. I needed six hours to complete my seminary requirements. I decided on the course because I thought it would be good preparation for the ministry. I was assigned to Cook County Hospital in Chicago.

While working with patients, I was surprised to find that I learned more about myself than I did about the patients. I soon discovered that for most of my life I had been taught a theology of perfection. I learned that I had to be perfect, and that salvation was the result of what I did or didn't do. I had been living a theology of salvation by works and not salvation by faith.

During a group session with other students at the hospital I discovered that I could not save myself. No matter how many people I helped or how hard I tried, I still felt separated and estranged from God. My supervisor said, "Bittner, salvation is a free gift from God. The only thing necessary for salvation, for wholeness is confession. We are made whole by God's grace."

His words turned on a light inside me. There *was* a solution to my feelings of guilt and rejection—God's grace. It was not as if I had never heard of the grace of God. I knew the words. The difference was in the way my supervisor and the students accepted and loved me. I had opened myself up to them and to God. My experience with them made grace a reality for me. God truly was a gracious God. I had experienced him through these men who loved me.

I left the hospital that day feeling light, alive, and most of all, free. God's Son had made me free from guilt. This happened because I had learned to talk about the things in my past that had been bothering me. As a human being I had needed a human experience. Confession only to God was not enough. I needed to tell it to others. They forgave me. If they could forgive me, surely God would forgive me.

Many people in the church are just like me. They have not experienced the grace of God. They feel that they have to "work out their own salvation" by being perfect, and atone for their own sins as well as for the sins of others. Some feel they can pay for their sins by unconsciously becoming ill, because they feel they deserve to be ill.

Am I Very Sick?

Ten-year-old Lorie came in through the Emergency Room one night with a severe asthma attack. This was not the first time she entered the hospital in this condition. It had happened quite frequently in the past four months, in fact. Every time she needed a shot of Adrenaline to be able to breathe normally. Usually she was able to go back home with her parents within an hour or so. This time the doctor planned to make some tests in the hope of finding a more effective medication.

The physician also suspected that Lorie's parents might be part of the problem. He requested the chaplain to see Lorie and her parents and to inform him what he had uncovered. Sometimes this is done because a chaplain is less threatening to a patient and family than a doctor or nurse.

Lorie was frail but alert. I introduced myself and told her that the doctor had asked me to stop by to see her. I asked her if she was feeling better today.

"Oh, yes," she said, "but am I very sick?"

"No, you're not *very* sick, but you are sick and your doctor thought that I could help if I talked to you. Is that okay?"

"Sure. But how is that going to help?"

"Well, maybe you can tell me something about yourself."

As she talked I observed that she was a very intelligent and sensitive little girl. She told me she had a younger brother and sister. She described how she and her seven-year-old brother had difficulty getting along. She said she felt bad about this. She told me how her mother and father got into fights, and how she felt that she and her brother were to blame for her parents' fighting.

I asked, "Do you feel it is your fault that your mother and father fight so much?"

She thought for awhile and said, "If I were a good girl Mother wouldn't be asking Daddy to leave."

I tried to explain that she was responsible for fighting with her brother, but she was not responsible for what her parents were doing.

Lorie, like some other children, felt guilty and responsible for her parents' marital problems. It was as if she deserved to be sick, because she was such a "bad" girl. There seemed to be a direct relationship between her asthma attacks and her parents' marital disputes.

On the night before Lorie came to the hospital her parents had talked about divorce. She recalled how she had overheard her mother tell her father that she felt trapped and wanted out. Her asthma attack came shortly after that had happened.

Like Lorie, many people feel they deserve to be sick. She had interpreted her parents to say that she was responsible for their marriage. They had never used those words, but this had been her understanding. Her guilt had not only brought on her asthma, but she saw her illness as a way of making up for being a "bad" girl. Illness for her was a way of getting rid of her guilt. In her young, subconscious mind she believed that the only freedom from guilt was punishment. She deserved to be sick. Only in illness would she find relief from her guilt.

I related this to the parents and suggested that

they come for marriage counseling. They did, but Lorie's mother was unwilling to work on her part of the problem. They eventually got a divorce.

I don't know if Lorie is still feeling responsible for her parents' mistakes. I can only hope and pray that her mother was able to help Lorie see that the marriage problem was not Lorie's responsibility, and furthermore, that she does not deserve to be sick.

Lorie's story shows how the feeling of guilt can be very destructive of bodily health. Guilt can be the primary cause of certain illnesses. There are times too when guilt is one of the factors that prevents people from getting well, along with denial and anger. The following story shows how guilt contributes to illness.

If Only

Larry, in his late twenties, was the father of two children. For some time he had been treated for a skin problem, and now he was admitted to the Crisis Intervention Unit with the diagnosis of acute depression.

One of the chaplain's functions on this unit is to conduct group therapy every day with all the patients who are enough in touch with reality to be able to benefit from it. The chaplain as well as the rest of the team (nurses, social workers, therapists, and psychiatric technicians) are encouraged to work with those patients with whom they relate well, or with those the psychiatrist thinks could benefit from their particular expertise or approach (mine being the psycho-religious aspect of health).

I suspected that Larry was angry at something because depression is usually the result of anger turned in on one's self. Later I found that he was really angry at himself and that this was just another way of saying that he was feeling guilty.

Larry's guilt was related to his father's death. His father had died unexpectedly about six months prior to Larry's hospitalization. Following that, he developed a skin problem and had gone to a dermatologist to get some relief, but it had become worse.

I asked the nurse to bring Larry to my office so I could have some time alone with him. I began by asking him to tell me about his father because I had the feeling that there might be some connection between his depression and the death of his father.

I asked if he would begin by telling me about his father's death. He told me how his father and mother had decided to go on a trip and how happy he was that they could go.

"But," he said, "I couldn't even take them to the airport. I was unable to take off from work. *If only I* had taken off and driven him to the airport I would have seen him before he left, before he died. If only *I* had taken him. If only. . . ."

"You sound as if you feel guilty because you didn't see him before he died. Did you have some unfinished business with your father?"

"What do you mean?"

"Tell me about your relationship with your father."

He told me that as a child he was never able to please his father. No matter how well he did anything it was never good enough. He recalled how he had grown to resent his father because he didn't feel accepted by him.

"And now you feel guilty because you didn't resolve your relationship with your father before he died."

"Yes, I do."

He began to weep. I walked over to him and placed my hand on his shoulder. I wanted him to know that I cared about him, that I was trying to understand.

"Larry, do you see that it's natural for a son to resent his father for not accepting him? Especially when he wants so much to be accepted by him and tries as hard as you tried to gain his approval."

"But I didn't have a chance to tell him that I loved him before he left!"

"Are you saying that you didn't ever tell him that you loved him?"

"Yes."

"I am sure you would have felt better if you could have told your father that you loved him. But how could you when you resented him? Do you think you have forgiven your father for not loving you the way you deserved to be loved?"

"Yes, I have. I know that I have. I know that he was just like his father. I remember my mother telling me about how terribly my grandfather treated him. I understand why he was the way he was and so I am able to forgive him."

"Then don't you think you had better forgive yourself?" I said. "The only prerequisite for forgiveness is confession, and you have made your confession. Accept God's forgiveness, or your guilt feelings will continue to make you sick!"

He was able to see that his depression came as the result of his feelings of guilt (anger at himself). Now that God had forgiven him, he no longer had to feel responsible for his father's death. Within a short period of time Larry was able to leave the hospital. Unfortunately, though, Larry had difficulty accepting God's forgiveness, because he had felt guilty and unacceptable for so long. Change takes time. In time the forgiveness of God will not only be an intellectual experience, but an emotional experience as well.

The situation of Larry illustrates that the feelings of guilt can cause illness and continue to prevent people from getting well. There are times, however, when guilt becomes the primary way in which people react to being ill. Unfortunately, some see illness only as the motivating force for feeling guilty over the unresolved real or neurotic guilt of the past. The next experience shows how one person's illness had no more meaning than to cause her to feel guilty.

If We Confess Our Sins

I was making presurgical rounds the night before surgery. The surgery list indicated that my next patient was scheduled to have a "D & C; possible hysterectomy."

Barbara was a middle-aged woman and I could see that she was quite anxious. She had been watching TV. As we began to talk I became aware of just how nervous she was. She was completely unaware of the program she was watching.

I asked her if she would tell me what kind of surgery she was having, even though I knew. I wanted to see what meaning the surgery had for her.

She answered my question correctly and then proceeded to tell me how frightened she felt. I told her that it was normal to be afraid, but that I wondered why it was that she seemed excessively frightened.

Then Barbara told the story of her unhappy, rather meaningless life. She had been reared in a Christian home and "had been taught what was right and wrong." Somehow things had gone from "bad to worse" and she had lived the life of a prostitute. She told me that she felt extremely guilty about this, but that she had been trapped in this life style. She had convinced herself that this was one way to feel loved, even though it wasn't fulfilling. But the more involved she became in this way of life, the more guilty she felt. And the more guilty she felt the more she needed to be loved. It was a vicious circle and there seemed to be no solution. And now she was going to have surgery. She was certain she would not live through the surgery.

"You mean," I said, "you feel that you don't deserve to live?"

"Yes; I know that God punishes us for wrongs, and I sure deserve to be punished. I hate myself for what I have made of my life."

"Who do you think is punishing you the most right now?"

"I guess I am. But doesn't God punish us? I have always heard, even as a child, that God will destroy the wicked. And I feel wicked."

She burst into tears. I was beginning to think that she was feeling more than she could handle. I was hoping that somehow I would be able to help her resolve this before her surgery tomorrow morning. A part of me was feeling anxious because I had allowed her to talk about this right before surgery. Another part of me was feeling good because she needed to dispel the idea that she deserved to die; otherwise she *might* die.

"I know you feel wicked, but so did the 'woman at the well.' Do you remember that story?"

"No, I don't."

I told her the story about the Samaritan woman from whom Jesus asked a drink of water. I told her about the conversation Jesus had with her as recorded in John 4. Jesus had asked her to go and get her husband, but she had said, "I have no husband." I explained that the woman of Samaria was admitting that she had many men. Yet, Jesus accepted her, because she was honest and confessed her sin to him.

I tried to help her to see that she had done the same thing with me and to God. She had confessed her sin. Then I said; "In the name of Christ, I forgive you."

For the first time, in our brief experience together, a calmness came over her. She had emptied herself of the guilt feelings that distressed her. Now she was relieved of the pressure to be perfect, of the need to be her own justification through punishment, and also from a life style of sin that had separated her from God. Through confession she had found an answer to her guilt and anxiety. She had begun to experience "the peace which passes all understanding," the peace only Christ can give.

Illness for Barbara had taken on a new significance. Her illness no longer caused her to feel guilty about her past. Her illness had created the crisis she needed to decide to do something about her spiritual sickness. Being ill had given her the opportunity to free herself from the guilt and shame of the past. Through confession she had discovered the forgiveness of God. Being sick had made it possible.

Her illness had counted.

Lord, it's great to be free from the *neurotic* guilts of life—
The shame that I feel, which I shouldn't feel.
The guilt I feel which is not realistic guilt—
But only a fantasy of the past.

Lord, it's great to be free of the *real* guilts of life
That cause the sadness to overwhelm,
And the despair to blind,
Because my view of you was too small.

Lord, it's great to be free from the guilt of sin,
The sin that I willfully committed,
    either by commission or omission.

Because of my inadequate, insecure feelings,
Because my needs were greater than my insight.
Because I trapped myself in a vicious cycle,
And I didn't see that you had the answer to my dilemma.

Lord, I know that you have made me free—
Free from the guilt of the past,
So that I can be free ...
For my responsibility.

Amen

4

WHAT WILL I DO NOW?

So we know and believe the love God has for us. God is love, and he who abides in love abides in God, and God abides in him. In this is love perfected in us, that we may have confidence for the day of judgment, because as he is so are we in this world. There is no fear in love, but perfect love casts out fear. For fear has to do with punishment, and he who fears is not perfected in love. 1 JOHN 4:16-18

One of the most paralyzing of life's painful feelings is fear. I recall how devastating my feeling of fear was as a child. I was seven years old. My mother was sick, how sick I didn't know. I believed that she must be quite sick because we were called to the hospital. Shortly after we arrived I remember my father saying that my mother wanted to see us all for a few minutes.

I recall the scene as if it were yesterday. My mother held my hand, gave me a kiss, and told me that she didn't have very long to live and that she wanted all of us to trust the Lord as she did.

We left the room, and minutes later the nurse came out to say, "She's passed away." I wasn't really sure what that meant. But then I saw my father and my sisters begin to cry, and I knew.

I can't describe my feelings. I felt sick. I felt all

alone, and I thought to myself, "What will I do now? How will I be able to live without my mother?" I felt helpless, hopeless, and lost.

Those words of my mother seemed empty and meaningless then, but later her words became a significant part of my life. I believe my mother planted a seed. It was meaningless at the time and became buried in my subconscious mind, but it bore fruit. Where there is belief in God, God's love abides. And where there is love (God) there is no fear.

I know that others have had similar experiences, experiences in which they felt, "What will I do now?" Their illness or crisis in life seems so overwhelming that they are afraid to go on. The fear of what lies ahead wipes out whatever security they felt as a result of their relationship with God and others. Sometimes their fear is so great that they become ill. For many being sick is better than being afraid. Through their illness they find a haven, a respite, from the pain of being afraid of the reality and responsibility of a life that seems hopeless.

I Know I've Got Cancer

Ken was a handsome man 32 years old. He was referred to me as an outpatient by a staff physician. The doctor informed me that Ken had gone everywhere for help. He was bothered by an agonizing pain in his throat, and he was certain that he had cancer.

After a few minutes, I was quite sure that he was primarily psycho-religiously sick, that his illness was not organic in nature. I confronted him with this thought and then I asked him why he felt it had to be cancer.

He told me how painful it was and how the pain had bothered him so much that he had actually begun to isolate himself from other people.

Then I asked him to tell me about his personal life. He related how he had been living with a woman for some time now. Significantly the pain had begun shortly after he began living with this woman. I told him that perhaps there might be a connection.

He related that he wasn't very happy with her. She was demanding, selfish, and most of all it was against what he really believed was right.

"Do you want to do something about the relationship that you have with your friend?"

"Well, I tried before, but she made such a fuss that I couldn't leave her. I didn't want to hurt her."

"Hurt whom? I think you're afraid of being hurt yourself. How could she hurt you?"

"I don't know."

"Are you dependent on her?"

"Yes," he said.

"Would you tell me about your parents and more specifically about your mother?" He told me how possessive his mother was and how she had always taken care of him.

"It sounds to me as if you are so anxious about life that you need someone to take care of you," I said.

"Yes, I guess that's the way it is. I can't even make a decision and stick to it."

"You mean, you *don't* make a decision and stick to it," I said. "You could if you wanted to."

"But I need her. I can't take care of myself. This pain is terrible."

I tried to help him to see that his biggest problem was fear and anxiety. Because of his fear of life he had gotten himself into a situation that was destructive to him, not only emotionally but spiritually as well. Unfortunately, his dependency needs were so great that he wouldn't make a decision to leave her. The result of his indecision caused him to become anxious. But because of his frozen situation—his unwillingness to leave—his anxiety and fear developed to the point that it expressed itself somatically —he began to have pain in his throat. The more pain he had the more anxiety he had. And the more afraid and anxious he became the more pain he had and the more fearful he was to leave the situation.

His anxiety and fear about being independent and making decisions developed into somatic complaints. But he was getting a dubious advantage out of his throat pains. Because of his pain, he didn't have to face his anxiety about life. In fact, how could he possibly leave this woman as sick as he was? He felt helpless, hopeless, and out of control, because he was afraid to grow up. His fear had made him sick and his illness had made him afraid. He was trapped in a vicious cycle.

I continued to see Ken a few times after that, but it was evident that he did not want to change. Apparently, the fear of facing life was so great that he would rather endure the belief that he had cancer. He eventually refused to come back. A short time later I heard that he became so anxious and withdrawn that he was hospitalized. His diagnosis was "anxiety reaction."

Ken was so afraid of life that he had in effect chosen illness. He was unwilling to allow God or man to help him.

There are times, too, when fear causes people to be sick, because they have not learned any other method of coping with their destructive feelings.

My Parents Don't Even Love Me

John was an 11-year-old boy who had already developed an ulcer. His parents had taken him to an internist for treatment. The internist referred him to me after giving him medication and a diet.

When they called for an appointment I insisted on seeing both parents with their son. It was obvious that the boy was having problems because his parents were on the verge of a divorce. He was so afraid that they were going to get a divorce that he had become sick. Unfortunately he had not found a healthy way to express his anxiety. When he would try to do it by being active he was reprimanded for being too noisy. He could find no other way to express his anxiety. There was no place for his fear to go, but to attack the weakest part of his body. The result was an ulcer.

I told the parents that their difficulties had resulted in their son becoming ill. The cause of their son's fear could be eliminated if he knew for sure that they were either going to work at their marriage or separate.

They decided to work at it, but they were both

unwilling to make the necessary changes. My counseling with them became counseling for divorce instead of marriage counseling.

After their separation John was no longer torn by the fear of what was going to happen with his parents. The fear of not knowing is much worse than knowing. Now his mother was able to use her energy to love her son, instead of using it in conflict with her husband. She was able to love John the way he deserved to be loved.

Previously, John had not received love from either parent. In addition, the insecurity of the home situation caused him to feel that he needed even more love and attention, but his parents were too preoccupied with their own problem to recognize his needs. There was no solution for John's fear, except to become ill. Unfortunately, the more discomfort he had with his stomach the more anxious and afraid he became. Not only was his illness caused by fear, but his illness resulted in his becoming more fearful.

With the marriage situation settled through separation, John's fear was replaced by the love of his mother and the resultant absence of tension at home. There is no fear in love, but only in the absence of love.

Both Ken and John had become ill because they were living with unresolved fears about life. There are also people who see nothing more in their experience of being sick than that it is something to be avoided because it is such a fearful experience. The primary focus for them is that illness is a terrible, awful, and most of all, fearful encounter. The following account is an example.

God's Love Casts Out Fear

I was awakened by the ringing of the telephone. It was the switchboard at the hospital. In my dazed frame of mind, I could hear the operator telling me that they needed a chaplain on 6 North.

At the desk I was told that one of the patients who was to have surgery tomorrow was very upset. She was scheduled for a conization, which is the cutting away of cervical cancer tissue.

The nurse told me that the patient was only 28 years old. Two weeks ago her doctor had discovered a change in her Pap smears. He had diagnosed it as cervical cancer. What made it more serious was that she was four months pregnant. She was aware that it was especially bad to develop cancer during a pregnancy. She knew that the chances of spreading were much greater during this time because there was considerable cell growth already occurring within her.

Christine had one child, but she wanted more. Through the conization her doctor hoped to deal with the cancer and not have to terminate the pregnancy.

"I'm afraid that I might lose my baby," she said. "I'm so nervous, I—I don't know what to do with myself."

I suggested that it might be better to go to another room so that we wouldn't disturb the patient in the next bed. She agreed. As we walked down the hall,

I put my hand on her shoulder in an attempt to comfort her and let her know that I was concerned.

"It's really very hard to think about the fact that you might lose your baby. But it seems to me that you are worrying about something that may not happen."

"I know that's true, chaplain, but that doesn't seem to help. You see, I have all these thoughts going through my mind."

"Try to tell me what you mean, will you?"

"I'm smart enough to know that surgery is no guarantee of success and it is not necessarily a protection against recurrence of cancer. I wish I knew what was going to happen. Then at least I would be able to know what I'll be up against. I think of the possibility of it not being a success, and then I think of the pain of losing my baby, the pain that might be involved in the illness, and even the pain of leaving my little boy and my husband. It's so frightening!"

"What do you mean, *it's* so frightening?"

"All of it!!!" Christine said angrily, and she began to cry.

"Yes, I know all of it's frightening, but of all the things that you mentioned, what is the most frightening of all to you?"

"I don't know," she said.

"I know you don't *know*," I said. "If you did know you wouldn't need to talk about it. But what do you think?"

"I guess it's the last one—leaving my family and. . . ."

"And . . . ," I said.

"Dying. I'm afraid of dying and I don't want to die. I have too much to live for!"

"No one wants to die. I don't want to die either, and I'm afraid of dying too. It's natural to be afraid," I said. "But what is the most frightening thing for you about dying? Is it being all alone?"

"Yes. Yes, that's it. I guess that's the one thing that everyone has to do alone, isn't it? Even as a child I knew that death was a certainty for everyone. But I didn't think it would happen so early."

"I'm feeling good and bad about what you said. Good, because you are saying that the death is a reality for us all, but bad because it sounds like you are dead already. You're not, you know!"

"I'm sorry. I didn't mean to sound like that. I guess I'm trying to face the possibility of death now, because that's what's making me so frightened. I've always believed in God, but somehow now he seems to be so far away. It's hard to believe that God loves me, especially when he allows this to happen."

"I'm sure it is," I said. "But even though God seems to be far away, he isn't. God is right here. He is as close to you as I am."

I took her hand and held it, and I said, "You see, just as I'm holding your hand now, God, too, is holding it. He'll be with you. He'll walk with you; he'll hold your hand so that you will know that you are not alone. God loves you and where Love is, there is no fear."

"You mean, if you care about me, God is present in your caring about me and there isn't anything to be afraid of."

"Yes, that's what I mean. You see, our Lord promised that when two or three are gathered in his name, he is there, too."

Her surgery was successful. However, two weeks later she lost her child. But one year later she became pregnant again, and after giving birth to her second child she had a hysterectomy to reduce the possibility of cancer.

She had faced the greatest human fear, the fear of death. Through her illness she had discovered that God is love and where there is Love, there is no fear. For her, illness had taken on a new meaning.

She had made her illness something to be feared; but now it had become the vehicle by which she had discovered how her knowledge of the love of God could help her to overcome fear, even the fear of death. She had made her illness count.

Lord, there are times when I am afraid of life:
I'm afraid of the pain of illness,
  of change,
  of not knowing,
  of leaving those I love, and
  of dying.
And Lord, I'm even afraid of being dead.

Sometimes I am overwhelmed by fear.
I need you and an important Other.
I need to experience your love through the love
  of another—another who cares.

Lord, help me to face my dying
  so that I don't trap myself,
  so that life is not hopeless,
  so that I don't feel helpless.

Lord, give me the wisdom
  to see you as a God who cares,
  who understands,
  who is trustworthy,
  who will never forsake me,
  and who will heal me for life and for eternity.

Lord, thank you for the gift of faith,
  the faith that makes it possible
  to know that God is love and
  to know that where there is love there is no fear.
For "perfect love casts out fear."

5

BUT I'M SICK!

> *And as he sat at table in the house, behold, many tax collectors and sinners came and sat down with Jesus and his disciples. And when the Pharisees saw this, they said to his disciples, "Why does your teacher eat with tax collectors and sinners?" But when he heard it, he said, "Those who are well have no need of a physician, but those who are sick. Go and learn what this means, 'I desire mercy, and not sacrifice.' For I came not to call the righteous, but sinners.*   MATTHEW 9:10-13

When I entered college I was not certain what I wanted to do with my life. I was inclined toward two different directions—being a coach or being a pastor.

By the end of my sophomore year I had decided to prepare myself for the ministry. I knew that as a pastor I would have to be able to preach. I couldn't think of anything more frightening than that. How would I possibly be able to get up in front of people and talk? I had trouble enough talking to *one* person. But hundreds? The very thought of it was devastating.

My intentions were good, however. In my junior year I decided to take some speech courses. If I was going to preach, I would have to learn how to give a speech.

I remember it well. It was my turn. Already on the day before, I was as "hyper" as one could get without hanging from the ceiling. The night was filled with restless sleep. Frequently it was interrupted by awakening out of awful nightmarish dreams, dreams of feeling trapped and of finding no way out.

The morning came early. I was awakened abruptly with a tremendous urge—it was diarrhea. I felt so much out of control in having to give my speech that I had become sick. But in the process of becoming sick I had gained control. My illness had given me power over my hopeless situation. Now I was able to justify the avoidance of giving my speech. Who could possibly expect anybody as sick as I was to get up in front of 35 fellow students and give a speech? And when my roommate reminded me that today was *my* day, my response was: "But I'm sick!"

I recall that giving my speech the next time was even harder, but I decided from that point on not to use being sick as a way of avoiding responsibility, no matter how sick I was.

Just as I became sick because I felt that I no longer had the power to be in control of my life, so do others. There are others, too, that use their illness as I did to control the unpleasant things in life. For some, illness becomes the means to manipulate and control the people and the environment around them. Illness becomes a means of power by which they try to avoid reality and responsibility for their own lives.

When we do this, we are looking for power in

things that don't give us power. If we realize that our real power is in God we will have the openness to see some value in things as difficult to face as illness. It is only by accepting our dependency on God and admitting that we need to change some of our sinful and destructive behavior that illness has any real value for life. As Matthew puts it, Christ did not come to save (to make whole) those who don't admit to needing any help. He came for those who are willing to repent, who want to live a more meaningful life, both here and eternally. The following illustration is an example of one who was afraid to give up the power she had gained through being sick, because she was using her illness as a way of coping with failure.

What Can You Expect?

Jan had come into our hospital with a severe case of colitis. I had been called in to see her by one of the physicians because he thought that she was not helping herself to get well.

She was an attractive woman of 22. My first impression of her was that she really didn't want to talk to me. She felt the way most of us do when we are depressed. What we need to do most of all is talk, but we find that the hardest thing to do.

I introduced myself and discovered that she was a student nurse. Things were not going well for her. A week ago she had been warned by her teachers that unless she began to do better on her tests and with her field assignments she might be asked to drop out of the course.

She told me what a terrible blow it was to hear that. She already had stomach problems and this made things worse. She had been taking medications and watching her diet, but with this added stress her colitis had gotten out of control.

I asked if anything else was bothering her.

"Well, there is. You see, it's my mother and father. My father has a drinking problem and he has been real bad again. My mother is trying for the fourth time to get him into a hospital for treatment. This has made her a mess. I'm not living at home but it still bothers me."

"I'm sure it does," I said.

"I guess that situation has bugged me all my life. Our home has always been in such an uproar that it has been impossible for me to concentrate on anything. It seems like everything I do ends in failure because I am always preoccupied with the way things are at home."

"You're angry at your father and maybe your mother, too, for allowing it to happen. But it seems to me that your anger is making you sick."

"I guess it is, but I don't know what to do about it. And besides, how can I be expected to do anything about my education if I'm sick?"

"You can't," I said, "until you get well. I don't know exactly how to say this, Jan, but I believe your illness has come at a convenient time for you. I think you want to be sick because you are so angry at your parents. Being sick is a way of getting back at your parents for what they have done to you, and it's also a way to avoid being responsible for your not making it in school. You are using your illness as an excuse for your failure in school."

"You mean my illness is a way for me to 'save face'? I think that's terrible! How can you say anything like that? You must think I'm an awful person."

"No, I don't think you're an awful person," I said. "I have difficulty facing responsibility too, at times. I would like to make others responsible for me. This is what I see you doing. What is bothering me most of all, though, is that you are destroying yourself, physically, by not resolving your anger, and psycho-religiously because you are not using your emotional and religious strengths to make use of your illness, but rather using your illness to avoid facing your responsibilities in school."

"I can see what you are saying and I know this has happened before, but what can I do about it?" she said. We talked about her immediate need, and that was to want to get well and for once in her life commit herself to succeed in her school work. She would have to stop using her illness as a means of coping with her failures in life. I also told her she had to get rid of her anger at her parents. This meant that she would have to forgive them.

Jan had used her illness as a way of outwardly being in control, when inwardly she felt out of control. It was her way of convincing herself that she was still in control of her own life. Unfortunately, she had made herself sick in the process.

Jan used illness as a power to superficially be in control of her life. Others use illness to control others. The following case is an illustration.

I Can't Do It Alone

Arlene was a 45-year-old stroke victim, mother of four children, referred to me by her physician. In the first interview she revealed that she was using her illness to "keep her husband." I soon realized that I would not be able to help her without seeing the whole family and especially her husband.

During my conversation with her and her husband, I discovered that their marriage had always been stormy. They had never really had a good marriage. Several times prior to her stroke they had talked about separation or divorce, but they had never carried out their threats, probably because they both needed their sick marriage. She needed to depend on him and *he* needed *her* to depend on him.

I knew that unless her husband changed, there would probably be no hope for Arlene to change. It was difficult enough for her to have to cope with the disappointing experience of the stroke which would naturally make most people dependent. She would need to be pushed by her husband if she was going to change.

"Do you understand why you are so dependent on your husband?" I asked.

"Well, if you had a stroke you would be, too. I can't get around alone."

I asked her husband if that was true. He told me that she was able to get around by herself, but she was afraid to try it alone. It was as if she were saying to him by her behavior, "If I get well, I will lose you. The only way that I can possibly keep you is if I remain dependent. The only thing that I have going for me is that I am sick. Being sick gives me control over my shaky marriage."

In spite of her husband's confrontation she refused to change. As far as I know she is still using her illness as a power to control her husband so that he will not leave her, and he is allowing her to do it.

Some individuals use their illness as a means of controlling their spouses so that they don't lose them. Others grow beyond that point because they are willing to change their destructive life style. In theological terms this is called repentance. The following story illustrates this.

Changed by Repentance

When I met Carl, he and his wife were having marital problems. They were a handsome couple in their middle twenties.

Shortly after I began to talk to them it became apparent that he was chemically dependent. He had quit using drugs, but was still abusing alcohol. I confronted him about this, but he was unwilling to admit that he had a problem. Instead, he became more defensive about it.

I suggested that they both go to visit a meeting of Alcoholics Anonymous and at least sit in on the five introductory sessions. After that, I suggested that he might be in a better position to make a decision.

They went to one meeting, but he refused to go back. I saw them several times after that and in our last session his wife decided that she would file for a divorce, because she thought that this sort of crisis was necessary for him to decide to change his destructive life style.

I did not hear from them for several months. Then one day I received a call. Carl wanted to see me. We talked for about an hour. It was apparent that he had decided to change. He agreed to join AA.

By this time his wife had decided she wanted out. When Carl heard this he was very upset. As is true for many alcoholics, he was going to AA to get his wife back. When he found out that she was going through with the divorce he became very despondent.

I tried to help him see that if he was going to have any success at changing his life around (repentance), he would have to do it for himself and not as a way to manipulate his wife to come back. He agreed with my premise but wasn't really committed to it. He verified this by continuing to remind his wife what he was doing. He told her how he was searching by reading Kahlil Gibran and by delving into the religion of Zen Buddhism. He wanted to feel that this was helping him, but inside he felt the gnawing realization that it wasn't. In continuing to tell her that he was changing, he was, in effect, trying to convince himself that he was getting his life put back together.

It is true that he was working at it, but he was doing it for the wrong reason, to get his wife back. He wasn't doing it because *he* wanted to change for himself. Later on he discovered that he was looking in the wrong places. He needed to come to terms with the Christian concept of repentance. This had been a part of his religious background but he had been rebelling against all of his past for some time and it was difficult to accept that not all of his past was negative. His exposure to Christianity had value even though his childhood was filled with broken and shallow relationships which caused him to feel unloved and insecure. He needed to stop trying to manipulate and control his wife and to start treating her as a person of value and worth. He needed to repent. This would be the only reason why she would want to come back.

All alcoholics have the conscious or subconscious desire to destroy themselves. This was still present in Carl. One night he decided to go to a party with some of his old drinking friends. He did not have anything to drink, but the fellow with whom he was riding had too much to drink. Carl knew it and tried to talk him out of driving home. The friend insisted that he would drive. Carl knew he should have gone home with someone else. On the way home they were involved in an accident. His friend was not hurt seriously, but Carl was paralyzed from the neck down. He was now a quadriplegic. How would he ever get his wife back now? He had nothing to offer her.

When his wife heard about it she came to him immediately. Carl was smart enough to know that if he could get his wife to feel sorry for him he might be able to get her back. It suddenly dawned on him that he had more power over her now than he had ever had during their marriage, and that was a lot. Before he had used his irresponsible behavior to control her; now he could use his illness.

This had played right into his old life style. He

was now able to "con" her into staying with him. How could she possibly turn him down?

Carl was right. Being a typical spouse of an alcoholic, she felt sorry for him. This was aided by her need to take care of people and this, too, was typical of most spouses of alcoholics. This is attractive to the alcoholic because he likes others to be responsible for him.

Carl had gained control over his wife again—in spite of his situation—and because of his situation. I felt that I had a responsibility to confront them both with what was going on in their relationship. If only I could get to his wife perhaps then we could get to him. If I didn't help her to see what she was doing, I knew that she would prevent me from getting to him. Fortunately, I was able to help her see what she was doing. She told him she would continue to love him, but she was not going to allow him to use his illness to control her.

When he began to get this message from his wife, he was quite belligerent and fearful. It was difficult for him to accept that his wife was going to love him just for himself and not because she felt sorry for him. But Carl's trust in God gave him the courage he needed to risk giving up the power he was trying to have over his wife. When he took that risk he found to his surprise that he didn't need to use his illness as a way to keep his wife. She loved him, because he was not trying to force her to love him by his use of self-pity. In fact, if he would have continued to do this, she would not have come back after their divorce was final. Instead they were remarried. Their life together became meaningful and happy.

Carl has become a successful businessman, only now he is using his disability as a means of being creative in designing and manufacturing innovative equipment to make the lives of other paraplegics more comfortable and productive. Illness for him is no longer a way of manipulating and controlling others. Illness provided the occasion for him to be able to accept his need for God and also his need to repent. Through his illness he is finding a more productive, meaningful life. His illness has given him the opportunity to change his life. He no longer needs his illness to control his wife. He has discovered that she can love him for being the person that God created him to be. And he loves her as a child of God, because his life has been changed.

Lord, forgive me if I use being sick as an excuse
   to avoid responsibility, or to cope with disappointment
   and failure.

Lord, forgive me when I use my illness to control the
   lives of others, and to gain power over those I love.
Sometimes I am so unsure of myself and so unwilling to
   admit that I need your power. Help me to know that
   through you I am able to change my destructive,
   manipulative ways.

Lord, thank you for your power that is free,
   the power that is mine when I admit that I am unable
   to be my own savior.

Lord, thank you for the power that makes repentance
   a possibility for me.
Without it I would be too scared to risk change,
   the change that makes life happy, productive, and
   meaningful.   Amen

6

IS ILLNESS
A WASTE OF TIME?

Rejoice in the Lord always; again I will say, Rejoice. Let all men know your forbearance. The Lord is at hand. Have no anxiety about anything, but in everything by prayer and supplication with thanksgiving let your requests be made known to God. And the peace of God, which passes all understanding, will keep your hearts and your minds in Christ Jesus.

PHILIPPIANS 4:4-7

When illness comes you are forced to accept the role of being sick. This is much easier said than done. You are forced to withdraw from many of the things you did as a healthy person. You give up making some decisions concerning your own welfare. You give decision-making authority to your physician and to your family. Society relieves you of some ordinary duties. You may not find this easy to accept. To give up your independence makes you feel inferior. You think you are a failure. You are overwhelmed and bombarded by a variety of feelings. Anger and guilt, fear and disbelief rise up inside.

Your feelings are further complicated by a desire to respond to your dependency needs. You may even wish to use your illness as a way of getting what you want.

Room 714

My telephone wakened me one morning at 2 A.M. The switchboard operator at North Memorial Medical Center informed me that a chaplain was needed on 7 North and connected me with a nurse at the station. "We are having trouble with Mrs. Mack in Room 714, Bed 1, Chaplain. How soon can you be here?"

I entered the room, introduced myself, and soon found myself confronted by 300 pounds of anger and hostility. Mrs. Mack said: "So they called a chaplain! Why did they want to bother you?"

"They didn't bother me," I said. "The fact that you are upset is important to the nurses and to me. That's why I'm here. How can I help you?"

Mrs. Mack was rather startled. She knew I had passed the test and that I was not going to be put off. She also knew I was willing to help her, so she began to talk.

She told me she was in the hospital because she had broken her leg. Prior to her hospitalization she had been living alone in an apartment even though she was not able to walk. When she was 19 years of age, the doctors had discovered that she had spinal cord cerebellum degeneration. The only way she was able to get around was by the use of a wheelchair, and now this had happened.

Mrs. Mack told me how angry and frustrated this accident had made her feel. "I can't understand why this had to happen to me. Haven't I had enough?"

Besides having this degenerative condition, she had recently been divorced from her husband who didn't know what responsibility meant. Prior to her marriage to this man, she had given birth to a son. The child's father had also been irresponsible. In addition, her child was retarded and had to be placed in a foster home because she wasn't well enough to care for him.

As she talked, she continued to wonder why she had no answers. "Why am I sick? It doesn't make any sense." The only thing she could see her illness had done for her was to give her a desire to avoid life—to be unfriendly and hostile toward others, to feel alone and cut off from people, to have an overriding feeling of anxiety and fear about whatever she did, and to use her illness to get attention from me and others. Her illness had no significant meaning for her life.

During our conversation, I tried to point out to her that she was not accepting her illness. One way she tried to avoid the reality of her illness was by having had a child. When she talked about this she said, "Nobody can say I have never been a mother!" Not only was Mrs. Mack trying to deny her illness, but she was saying that even though she had an illness she was valuable because she had given birth to a child.

In my subsequent conversations with her I could see that she also had feelings of anger and resentment. I told her that her anger and resentment were destructive because she was using them to deny her illness. She was also isolating herself from others. I wanted her to see that she needed to resolve her anger over having had an abnormal child and not being able to care for him. She also needed to give up her anger about her illness and her anger at her immature husband who had misused her throughout their marriage.

She was also burdened by feelings of guilt because she had a child outside of marriage. A part of her guilt came from the resentment she felt toward her parents, because her illness was hereditary and she knew that she shouldn't resent them for this. Guilt usually follows resentment that is unjustified. Her guilt was further exaggerated by the failure of her marriage. If only she had been more rational and had acted more maturely, she said, her insecurities would not have drawn her into a bad marriage.

I wanted to help her with her guilt, but I knew that she could not resolve her guilt until she resolved her anger. I was concerned because her anger and guilt caused such an overwhelming feeling of anxiety and fear that she was afraid to try anything to change her destructive attitudes.

In her constant state of anxiety she learned that eating provided momentary relief. In the process she had become a "foodaholic" who weighed nearly 300 pounds. But eating was only a temporary solution to her anxiety. The more she ate the more she disliked herself, and the more she disliked herself the more anxious she felt, and the more anxious she felt the more she ate. She was caught in a vicious cycle, but this cycle had a "pay-off": she used it to manipulate others. Because she was getting something out of being sick she was not motivated to do anything about her destructive attitudes. If she changed she would have to stop using her illness to control others.

The sense of power and control she gained from her illness was difficult to give up. If she gave this up, she wondered how she would get anyone to pay attention to her. After all, she was sick and was convinced that she was of no value to anyone. I tried to help her see that if she chose to do something about her destructive thinking and behavior, she would be a more likable person. Unfortunately, this was difficult for her to comprehend, because she had discovered that she was getting attention by having a poor attitude, being hard to manage, and putting other people down. After all, hadn't it worked with me? Using her tactics she was able to get attention in the middle of the night.

Although a part of her wanted to be well, a part of her wanted to be sick. Because of her foodaholism and her unwillingness to exercise she had lost the ability to walk. Her immobility enabled her to gain the sympathy and pity of others and to get her own way. Her illness was a means of controlling others and making others responsible for her.

I saw Mrs. Mack several times while she was hospitalized, but because of her unwillingness to change her destructive attitudes she found no meaning in her illness. Even her religious resources were of no value to her. She refused to accept her illness and avoided the responsibility for her attitudes that were making her physically, emotionally, and spiritually ill.

It Was a Waste of Time

As far as I know, Mrs. Mack found no meaning in her illness. When I saw her again less than a year later, she was still denying, still angry, still feeling her shame and her guilt, still succumbing to fear and anxiety by overeating, and still using her illness in a manipulative way to control others. Because she has never been able to grasp the idea that there is meaning in illness, she is unwilling to accept the reality of her illness. She has not realized that there is still meaning to life in spite of illness, and that an ill person can still live her life to the fullest degree.

For Mrs. Mack, illness was a waste of time. She had denied her capacity to function as a human being. She had denied herself the opportunity for God to give any meaning to her illness. She had denied her freedom to decide by deciding not to decide, and by giving up. She had denied her potential to be responsible for herself by manipulating others and even trying to manipulate God into being responsible for her.

What had happened to develop such a "sin-sick" attitude toward life? Her attitude was goalless, fatalistic, dependent, and inflexible. This attitude was the result of her unwillingness to accept responsibility for her own life because of her fear of failure, and her unwillingness to accept that she had the capacity to find meaning wherever she chose to find it—even in illness.

You can be a responsible person and a person who believes that things are possible if you are willing to be open to the power of God in your life. You will not be controlled by your illness. Rather you will find a purpose in it.

You may be thinking: "If he really knew the battle going on within me he would not be talking so glibly!" It is true that I do not know the extent of your physical and psycho-religious pain. Only you know that. I would be the last to say that pain is not real. But I also know that sometimes it seems much easier to hear sympathy regarding a predicament in life than to be confronted with what can be done about an illness. Most people do not want to hear anyone say that they can do something with their illness, and that they are the only ones who can give it any meaning. Receiving sympathy seems easier for the moment and becomes a way of continuing to deny the reality of illness, to avoid having to change destructive attitudes about it, and to begin the struggle of seeing its meaning for life.

The power of God gives hope to overcome denial, forgiveness to overcome resentment, confession to overcome guilt, faith to overcome fear, and repentance to overcome misusing illness to manipulate others. And because you believe in God, even if he seems to be far away at times, you will believe in yourself. You will believe that you have the ability to find meaning in illness if you are open to finding it. Allow God to help you to be willing!

The Lord is my shepherd: I shall not want.
Lord, that's a comforting thought. . . .
It's great to know that you will provide.
But it's hard to be sure. . . .
I'm sick!

He maketh me to lie down in green pastures;
He leadeth me beside the still waters.
Lord, what does this mean?

Does this mean that you will give me peace and calm
   for my life?
But my illness is making me anxious.
I don't want to be sick.

He restoreth my soul: He leadeth me in the paths
   of righteousness for his name's sake.
Lord, you will save me and make it all better!
But when? I'm burning inside.
How can it be righteous for me to be sick?
I'm angry, Lord.

Yea, though I walk through the valley of the shadow of
   death, I will fear no evil:
Lord, I know I'm not supposed to be afraid,
But how sick am I?
Will I die?
Lord, I'm afraid to die.

. . . For thou art with me.
Thy rod and thy staff, they comfort me.
Lord, I'm sick, anxious, angry, afraid,
And now, I feel alone.
Help me in my illness and isolation,
Lord, help me to know that you are here.

                                              Amen

7

I SURRENDER...

Be joyful always, pray at all times, be thankful in all circumstances. This is what God wants of you, in your life in Christ Jesus.

1 THESSALONIANS 5:16-18

During my seminary days I encountered a severe personal crisis. It became so encompassing for me that I found myself unable to concentrate on my studies. As a result of this, I dropped out of school. I had come to the point of questioning whether or not the ministry was for me. I began to separate myself from people and from God. God seemed to be far away. In fact, I began to wonder where God was. When a person isolates himself from people, he ends up isolating himself from God as well. I had forsaken God by separating myself from him; God hadn't forsaken me.

Some church members believe that all you need to do in such a situation is to "praise the Lord." If I had only praised the Lord more and "rejoiced" in everything, would my crisis have disappeared?

Good as such a religious motto may sound, it does not always work. To be sure, we are encouraged to

"Give thanks in everything: for this is the will of God in Christ Jesus concerning you." But this is very hard for us to do. When you face a personal crisis in your life, whether it be religious, emotional, or physical, it becomes difficult to say what you do not feel. This, of course, does not mean you have license to wallow in your negative feelings because that will result in self-pity, and self-pity is one of the most destructive attitudes we can have.

Our negative feelings must be faced honestly when they are present. Denial allows them to be destructive of ourselves and others as well. There are people in hospitals, for emotional and physical problems, because they have bottled up their negative feelings about life and even about God. For the Psalmist in a similar case, the saving (healing) thing was not that he began by praising the Lord. He began with what he was feeling at the moment. See Psalms 10, 55, 69, and 109.

If he was angry, depressed, afraid, distrustful, hopeless or helpless, he began there. He didn't begin by praising God. He was intelligent enough to know that the primary function of prayer was to establish a relationship with God. He also had enough wisdom to know this could best be done by beginning with God where he was, emotionally and spiritually.

For me, God worked a miracle. Providentially, my supervisor at work was a dedicated Christian man. (Two years after I finished the seminary he became a Wycliffe translator in South America.) He knew that I was a seminary dropout and asked me to come to a Bible study he and a few others conducted.

In my confused state of mind, I resented him for

inviting me, because I had isolated myself from God. I wanted nothing to do with God. I wanted to be left alone. Unfortunately, most of us don't feel like talking to anyone when we are hurting, but that is what we need most of all.

But he persisted. Finally God got through to me. I joined the Bible sharing group. The intimacy and prayer support of that small group of people led me to go back to the seminary. They had given me opportunity to share my hurts. They had accepted me enough to allow me to be where I was at the time. I was miserable, but I was able to change, *not* because I started by praising the Lord, but because I was allowed to verbalize my negative feelings. They loved me in spite of it, just as our Lord does.

Eventually, I finished seminary and entered the ministry. As I look back on that crisis experience, I am able to thank and praise God for it. At the time, it was like being in hell. I was estranged from God and had become an island unto myself. Now I realize such experiences enabled me to grow and mature as a Christian. A person's faith is never vital and alive unless it is challenged either by crises or by mountains to be climbed.

Just as I am able to look back at my personal crisis and be grateful for it, others are able to look back at the crisis of illness and praise God for it. If only more people would use illness as an opportunity for growth and maturity! Too many are unwilling to see illness as an encounter with a part of life they haven't met before. They don't want to see it as an opportunity for growth, but only as a waste of time they would like to avoid. They do not make their illness count.

Mary is an individual who was unwilling to use her illness constructively. Eventually she realized that she had to "grow up." Otherwise she would have continued to make herself physically ill and suffered an emotional breakdown or committed suicide.

Maturity Through Illness

The first time I met Mary was in the emergency room. She had come in with a bleeding ulcer. She had lost so much blood that she had passed out while working at home and had to be taken by our ambulance to the hospital.

Shortly after she arrived she became hysterical in the thought that she was going to die. The nurse had called our office for a chaplain.

After talking with her for a short period of time I became aware that she had difficulty handling her emotions in a constructive way, and that she was chemically dependent. We did not discuss this at the time, however, because my main concern was to assure her that she wasn't going to die. I tried to assure her that if she cooperated with the medical staff everything would be all right.

I told her that I would like to come back to see her after she got situated in her room and was feeling better. I wanted to help her with the cause of her ulcer, namely the inadequate and destructive way she was handling her feelings.

She agreed, and the next day I stopped by to see her. We talked about how she had always been taught as a child that she was to be "seen and not heard." Expression of feelings was forbidden. Mary had learned well not only from what her parents told her, but also from their example. They didn't express themselves to each other either. If there was an exchange of feelings it was done nonverbally.

Mary was also exposed to a neurotic way of handling problems and that was by using chemicals. When her father got angry, frustrated, *or happy,* he would "need" a drink. He needed a drink when he was angry or frustrated because the only way he could express how he felt was after he had been drinking. He needed a drink when he was happy because he "deserved" it.

As we talked she realized that she would have to change. Not only would she have to learn to express herself emotionally, but also she would have to do something about her chemical dependency.

At first she had trouble admitting that she was chemically dependent. She didn't think she was as bad as all that. She surely didn't think that she was an addict.

"What is an addict?" I said.

"Well, she is someone who is really hooked. She's —well, like she's on skid row."

"Less than 5% of the chemically addicted people are on skid row. All the rest are functioning just like you. Of that 5% on skid row, most of them are there for some other reason," I said.

She began to see that she didn't have to be a "bum" to be addicted. She could be a suburban housewife who had become hooked on Librium prescribed by her family physician. She could see that even though she was taking care of the house and the children after a fashion, she was drug dependent and abusing pills. She was living the fantasy that without tranquilizers she would not be able to function. By this I am not saying that she should never use tranquilizers. God created them, too. However, we should not abuse addictive medication.

Before she could accept any help from God or anyone else, she would first have to admit that she had lost control of her life. The way she was managing it was making her physically sick (ulcers), as well as psycho-religiously sick (addiction).

Admission of helplessness was difficult for her—as it is for all of us. None of us likes to admit that he can't take care of himself. When we admit we are helpless we open ourselves up to the realization that we need God. We need a strength, a courage, and a hope from someone outside of ourselves, who will never let us down.

If Mary had not been brought into the hospital almost dead with a bleeding ulcer she would never have discovered that her life was unmanageable and that she needed God to give it proper direction. Her illness became the opportunity to face herself and her problem and to grow and mature as a person.

Up to this point her life was empty and meaningless. What she needed to do now was to surrender her life to God. She had to admit that she was in need of his help to regain control of her life, not only to get well, but to find happiness.

The word *surrender*, for many, is like waving a red flag. For some people this word implies the giving up of one's freedom. This is not what it means at all.

Surrender is the commitment we make to God or to another person to open ourselves up for honest encounter and intimate sharing. It is the experience of being loved and accepted completely, but also the feeling of wanting to love and accept others. The latter is the most threatening, because sometimes we are hurt by people when we open ourselves up for intimacy and closeness—and none of us wants to be hurt.

Mary's surrender to God came months after her hospitalization. I continued to see her on an outpatient basis for some time. After several sessions we both agreed that I had done all that I could for her in therapy and she would have to do the rest herself.

Two months later, after my secretary told me that Mary had called to make an appointment, a rush of feelings went through me. Why was she coming back? I usually never hear from people when they're making it, only from people who are having problems. I hoped she hadn't had a "slip" and gone back to abusing chemicals.

On the day she walked into my office I could see that she had found what she was looking for. Her walk was vibrant and alive, her face was beaming, and she could hardly wait to tell me the good news.

"I found God," she said. "It has been such a long search. I can't tell you what pain I've gone through. It was midnight about a month ago and I was going through hell emotionally and spiritually. I had been talking on the phone to a friend of mine because I was so depressed.

"I was using all the energy I could muster to hold

on. I felt as though I just couldn't take it any more. Even though I didn't ever want to end up like my father (he committed suicide), I felt that ending it all was the only solution. I felt as though I was going to burst. I had told my friend that I was going to leave my husband and children. And I thought to myself, 'Boy, they'll be sorry!'

"I felt I had to scream or I would burst. I was standing in the middle of my kitchen floor and in despair and anger I swore at God. I told God I couldn't hang on any more. I pleaded with him that if I was going to kill myself or lose my mind that he should let it happen *now. I surrender. You do it, God!* I don't care any more. *You do it!'*

"I began to cry. I cried, and cried, and cried. I began to shake and momentarily I began to laugh somewhat hysterically. In a few moments a calmness came over me.

"But God *hadn't* done it. God hadn't either allowed me to kill myself, nor had I lost my mind. Rather, I had found a peace and an aliveness which I had never experienced before.

"This sounds really crazy, but I felt so exuberant that I wanted to do something—something physical —so I went bowling. Oh, I get down sometimes, but it doesn't last. And there is a calmness and a peace in my life that is constant.

"The reason I didn't come in right away is because I wanted to make sure it was real. I know I will still have some bad days, but I know now I'm not alone —God is with me. That night when I gave up and admitted I couldn't do it alone, I experienced a closeness to God that I had never felt before. Until then, I was afraid to surrender to God because I thought I would be consumed by him. I *am* consumed by God, not in a confining way, but by his love, and I am constrained, as Paul says, to love others. That's why I had to come to tell you.

"When you told me what I had to do—to stop taking drugs, forgive my parents and my husband, and forgive myself because God forgives me—I thought it was impossible. You made me furious, because you believed that I could do it. I did, but only because I had God's love, strength, and help."

Through the crisis of illness, Mary had found *life*. Her illness had counted for something. She had become a more mature parent and wife. She had discovered the graciousness of a God who will never forsake us. His grace enables us to be willing to be open and intimate with him. His grace makes us willing to surrender. She had given up trying to make it by herself. She found God. She found maturity.

Her illness counted.

Where are you, God?
Sometimes you seem far away—
so remote, so impersonal, so uncaring.

I know you're not this way, Lord,
    but when illness comes I feel like that.
I feel forsaken and forgotten,
    and I wonder where you are, or if you are.

You're with me.
And if I had been close to you before,
    I would have known that.
But I wasn't.
Forgive me!

But I am thankful, Lord.
    You have never forsaken me, nor will you.
I've experienced this in my illness.

Being sick helped me realize my need for you.
Without you I'm lost and out of control.

When I gave up trying to do it alone,
    when I surrendered my life to you,
I found love, openness, and maturity.
I found LIFE.   Amen

8

I'LL NEVER BE DISAPPOINTED

*Therefore, since we are justified by faith, we have
peace with God through our Lord Jesus Christ.
Through him we have obtained access to this grace
in which we stand, and we rejoice in our hope of
sharing the glory of God. More than that, we rejoice
in our sufferings, knowing that suffering produces
endurance, and endurance produces character, and
character produces hope, and hope does not disappoint us, because God's love has been poured
into our hearts through the Holy Spirit which has
been given to us.* ROMANS 5:1-5

Thanksgiving was only a few days away. We were
having our first snowfall of the year.

The snow was beautiful, but it was wet and heavy,
as it always is at that time of the year. The only bad
thing about snow is that sometimes it makes driving
treacherous and it requires shoveling, especially this
year because almost six inches had fallen.

When it stopped, I decided to do my duty and
shovel it so that I would be able to get my car into
the garage. I live on a hill so it is almost impossible to
get into the garage unless the driveway is shoveled.

Everything was going fine. I was enjoying myself.
It was good to be out in the beauty of nature. But a
pastor has many demands on his time, and as a result

I had let myself "go to pot." I hadn't learned how to discipline myself to take time for exercise.

Even worse than not having had any physical exercise, I was 35 pounds overweight. And "blimps" don't shovel driveways very well. Everything physical becomes a chore. I kept telling myself, if only these women in my church weren't such good cooks, I wouldn't have this problem. Of course, I knew none of them had shoved the food down my throat and no one had twisted my arm either. I simply was an undisciplined slob. I had not taken care of my body.

I was getting to the end of the driveway. Up until then I had done well in spite of my plump physique. All of a sudden a tremendous pain pierced my lower back. I tried to straighten up but I couldn't. I was stuck at a 45 degree angle and it seemed almost permanent.

Within two hours I was in the hospital. Little did I know that my romp in the snow would end like this. I was feeling depressed and angry for not taking better care of myself. My doctor didn't help any either. He told me I had to lose 35 pounds or it would probably happen again and I had to get some physical exercise.

The first day I had a good case of self-pity and I was feeling like a martyr. I had been working so hard for the Lord and look what I had received for it—a hospital bed.

As the week progressed, I rather enjoyed my stay. I had needed a rest. I had needed a warning about the way I was abusing my body with food and inactivity. And those back rubs were great! I needed them more than anyone else. *I did have a bad back.*

I began to feel grateful for my illness, for my time in the hospital and my months of recuperation. In spite of the pain, the interruption of my daily life, and the long recuperation, I had become wiser.

I no longer had to solve everyone's problems, or eat everyone's cooking. I had learned that my value to God was not in being a foodaholic or a workaholic, but in who I am as a person. And my value as a person demanded that I care for myself and take some time for my own re-creation. My value was no longer based on my accomplishment with work or food. Now my peace of mind could come from accepting that I am justified by faith and that my hope for sharing in the glory of God was dependent on my Lord's grace and nothing else. And besides, if the basis of my hope was in God and not in my accomplishments, I would never be disappointed. Wisdom for me had come in an unusual way. This insight had come through my illness.

Now, I realize that you who read this may feel that it's easy for Bittner to say that he is grateful for his illness, because through it he was able to find some wisdom for his life. But what is a back problem compared to being paralyzed or waiting to die? I agree, a back problem is nothing compared to what you may be going through. Only you know how hard it is to face your illness.

But don't block yourself from seeing the truth in this, especially as it applies to your situation. The following example will help illustrate what I mean.

Suffering Produces Wisdom

The first time I met Grant was when I was making pre-surgical rounds. He had come in for tests that required anesthesia. He had been noticing a change in his bowel movements. He told me he had read that this was one of the indications of cancer. He had also noticed blood in his stool on several occasions.

For a long time he had tried to ignore it. He was aware of how anxious he had become, how impatient and irritable he was with his two children, and also how much his relationship with his wife had recently deteriorated.

About a week before, he and his wife were having a disagreement over the discipline of one of their children. He felt that the discipline should be more severe and his wife had disagreed.

The conflict was over a small issue, but before they realized it they were involved in a full-blown war. No partner ever wins a war. Both are losers. But sometimes things have a way of getting out of hand before you know it. He had become so angry that he lost control and slapped his wife. He had never done that before. No matter how angry he was, and no matter what she had done, she didn't deserve that. She hadn't done anything. She had only disagreed with him.

He felt terrible. He felt ashamed and guilty and isolated from her. Fortunately, his wife knew him well. She knew that he had never been this upset before. She was wise enough to know that something else was bothering him.

Because they had enjoyed a good relationship up to now, and had always been able to talk things out, she could tell him that she felt something else was bothering him.

He remembered how angry and threatened that had made him feel. He responded by lashing out at her even more, but she loved him enough to take it. Finally, it dawned on him that his physical condition had become such a concern for him that he was handling it by being angry and impatient with his wife and family. In that situation he had relearned the importance of talking. He had rediscovered the truth that many times a person doesn't know what he is thinking and feeling until he talks about it. As someone said, "I don't know what I feel; I haven't said it yet!"

He told her what had been happening, how he had found blood in his stool and how worried this had made him. That night he promised himself and his wife that he would telephone his doctor the next day. This resulted in his coming into the hospital.

I told Grant I would be back to see him the next day to find out what showed up in the tests. I knew he might have some trouble facing any bad news alone. Anyone would, but especially he, because he was only 30 and had two small children.

Later that afternoon, I received a call from a physician on our staff. On his rounds he had stopped in Grant's room and Grant had mentioned that he had talked with me. The doctor wanted to know if I would like to go with him to the room because the news was bad. The diagnosis was cancer of the colon.

I felt good about the doctor asking me to go with him, and especially about this doctor because he was aware that a person's spiritual health is an important factor in recovery. This doctor was a dedicated Christian himself and we had worked together before.

To tell a person about cancer is never an easy task. There is no gentle way of breaking this news. The important thing is to tell him the truth and then be there to help him in any way you can. This was what we would do, because this physician was convinced of his moral obligation to tell his patients the truth. Grant had trusted him enough to go to him for tests. Didn't he have the right to hear the facts?

The doctor told him what he had found and what they would do to try to correct it. He told Grant he couldn't guarantee anything, because the only way they would know the extent of the cancer was to perform surgery.

Grant was noticeably upset. The three of us talked for a while. Grant expressed his feelings of apprehension. We tried to let him know this was normal and then we tried to use whatever spiritual and emotional resources Grant had for strength and comfort. We told him we would like to pray with him. We formed a circle by holding each other's hands. The doctor was on one side of the bed and I was on the other. Each of us prayed in our own way.

I will never forget that experience. There was a special sense of community and oneness in Christ. This kind of experience makes life take on a vitality that dispels the sadness that is often a part of the life of a patient, a doctor, or a chaplain.

The next morning I visited him again just before he went to surgery. I shared a few poignant moments with Grant and his wife. They fluctuated between faith and uncertainty, and between tears and calmness.

The surgery took longer than expected. Not only did the doctor have to perform a colostomy, which is a surgical opening between the colon and the surface of the body, but he had had to remove almost one-half of Grant's colon. He would have to spend about one month in the hospital allowing a special process to work. A piece of iron pipe had been inserted in his colon to help the remaining sections grow together.

The month of Grant's recovery was very difficult. His doctor had told him he was not certain how well things would go even after he left the hospital. He might or might not be able to get along quite well. If not, he might not have long to live, six months to a year at the most. For certain, Grant would have to go through the discomfort of having cobalt treatments.

While Grant was in the hospital I spent a great deal of time with him and with his wife. Two days after his surgery I decided to stop in to see him. It was late in the afternoon. His wife was with him. They were talking about what would happen to the two children if something happened to Grant.

Both Grant and his wife were asking the usual question—why? Most of the time it is as difficult for the spouse to accept as it is for the patient. I remember Grant questioning it because no one in his family had suffered cancer before. He was wondering where it had come from, and saying if something should happen to him, his wife would have a tremendous responsibility in caring for the children by herself.

I tried to help them to see that to ask "Why?" would not help them. There is no direct answer to that question. Rather, they would have to accept it. Both of them went through the usual process of trying to accept Grant's illness. There was the denial and the anger, the guilt and depression, the fear and isolation, and finally, the acceptance.

Even though Grant had accepted it, on some days he would revert back to being depressed, just as all of us have our ups and downs.

I remember the day Grant went home. It was a happy day. He had built up confidence and hope that everything was going to be all right. I was happy for him, even though I thought he was not being realistic about the possibility of the cancer's return, especially because his was a severe case and it had not been detected at the early stages.

Six months passed and I hadn't heard from either Grant or his wife. Then one day I received a call from his wife. She was noticeably upset and concerned. Grant had been having trouble again. He wasn't eating and he was nauseated most of the time. The doctor had recommended that he come into the hospital.

The day for his return to the hospital came. Those last few days were filled with a mixture of joy and tears, not only by Grant and his wife but also by the staff, his doctor, and myself. Grant lived for only two more weeks. The only thing that could be done for Grant was to make him as comfortable as possible. Toward the end he refused to take any medication, because he wanted to remain as alert as possible.

The day he died was bright and sunny. It was mixed with times of consciousness and sleep. At 8:00 P.M. the end came. He slept away. Two hours before he died he had a period of consciousness that lasted for about 15 minutes.

During this time he asked his wife to page me. I came immediately because I knew the end was near. He had something to say to his wife and he wanted me to be there.

"I know that I am going to die, and I have accepted it. A few days ago I would have had trouble because I had hoped for a miracle. Well, there was a miracle, but it wasn't the miracle I had anticipated. My miracle was the realization that my hope was not in having a longer life, but my hope is in Christ. I know death is a reality for everyone eventually. For me it has come too soon, but I can accept it because I have learned that if my hope is in Christ I will never be disappointed."

He took his wife's hand, and looked directly into her eyes and said, "I want you to know I'm ready, Dear." He closed his eyes and almost immediately fell into a deep sleep.

Grant had died. God hadn't healed him physically, but he had healed Grant spiritually and emotionally. Grant had experienced the miracle of healing. He had been granted the *wisdom* that many people never acquire, that if one's hope is in God, he will never be disappointed. Through his sufferings he had found "endurance, . . . character, . . . hope, and hope does not disappoint us." Through his illness he had experienced the love of God which is the only basis for hope that will not disappoint us.

Grant's illness had counted.

Wisdom, what is it, Lord?
Is it knowing how to make a million, or
    how to solve the energy crisis?
Is it knowing what it is that determines death legally,
    or when to pull the plug to end life?
Is it knowing when to prevent conception, or
    whether to terminate an unborn child?
Is it knowing when to do a transplant, or
    when to do open heart surgery?
What is it, Lord?

Or is wisdom to respect you, Lord—
    to know you as a living, gracious Father?
"Knowing that suffering produces endurance,
    and endurance produces character,
    and character produces hope,
    and hope (in God) does not disappoint us. . . ."

Thank you, Lord, for the joy of having wisdom,
    wisdom that hope in you will end all disappointment.

                                  Amen

9

A DOZEN YELLOW ROSES

*Yes, and I shall rejoice. For I know that through
your prayers and the help of the spirit of Jesus
Christ this will turn out for my deliverance, as it is
my eager expectation and hope that I shall not be
at all ashamed, but that with full courage now as
always Christ will be honored in my body, whether
by life or by death. For to me to live is Christ, and
to die is gain.* PHILIPPIANS 1:19-21

Many years ago, I once reached the point of thinking my life had become so empty and meaningless
that I decided to end it all. I felt so alone and isolated that I concluded the only solution was suicide.
In my sick way of thinking I was unable to find any
other solution to my problem. Life seemed hopeless,
and I felt helpless.

Fortunately, I was unsuccessful. Usually, when a
person is contemplating suicide, the most crucial
time is the first twelve hours. If he is able to get
beyond that, he usually will not do anything destructive to himself.

Ironically, this had happened the Saturday night
prior to Easter Sunday morning. In my confused
state of mind I found myself walking toward the
entrance of a church. Something inside of me was
pulling me toward that church. I hadn't thought of

it until this writing, but maybe it was the seed of faith my mother had planted years before. Back there in the hospital at age seven, she had told me that I shouldn't be afraid, that I should trust the Lord as she did.

That Easter Sunday was a glorious experience for me. It was not only the day on which Christians all over the world celebrate the resurrection of Christ, but it was a resurrection experience for me. Death had been so close to me because I had been immature and so filled with self-pity that I was unable to think of anything but myself. I was looking for an immediate solution to my problems. Immature people want to have things go their way, but mature persons are more willing to be patient. Mature people are less willing to believe that they are helpless and that life is hopeless. They want to allow God to help them help themselves. When people have fully realized that they can't make it alone, it is less difficult for them to give their lives over to God.

For the first time in my life Easter had become meaningful. My view of God no longer was obscured by my tunnel vision which had seen him only as a God of wrath and a God of "dos" and "don'ts." I saw him as a God of grace, forgiveness, and love. How had I missed this for so long? I had grown up in the church and had been in it for years, and I had missed it. I had missed it as so many others have missed it. There are many people in the church who have been a part of the church all their lives, but have missed the message that God is love. Oh, they have heard it, but they have not experienced it emotionally.

My experience with suicide was hell for me, but I will be eternally grateful for it. I hope I will never allow myself to get to that point again. I know it won't happen if I am open to people and to God. But even though it was hell, I now thank God for it, for without it I would never have known how much I needed God's help, nor would I have become aware of the need to surrender myself to him. And if I had not surrendered myself to God, I would not have had anything about which to rejoice. Nor would I have known the freedom God's forgiveness has brought me. Through this liberating experience I have found a new life for service. I have discovered that God's love and a recreated life is only experienced when a person is willing to risk giving his life over to God.

My experience with suicide has also given me an awareness of suffering people endure as I would never have had any other way.

One of the joys of a hospital chaplain is to conduct group therapy with people in our crisis intervention unit. Most of the people who come to this unit don't care about themselves. They express this by attempting to destroy themselves, either by drugs, alcohol, suicide, or antisocial behavior. A person wants to destroy himself because he feels that no one cares about him and he doesn't care about himself. I try to let patients in that predicament know that God cares and that I care. This may not mean much to them at the time, because they are too mixed up and confused. However, if they have any religious resources at all, this assurance can give them the impetus they need to want to get well, and people don't get well unless they want to get well.

Many patients who come to our crisis unit feel they are the only ones who are depressed, unhappy, or suicidal. When they get here, they are able to see that there are others who have similar problems.

They also have the feeling that they are different from the staff. They are sick and the staff is healthy. Unfortunately, the patients sometimes use this as a superficial reason not to trust the staff. The truth is, everyone is a little neurotic; the difference is only a matter of degree.

The patients also have the feeling that the staff does not understand them. In this area I believe I have something special to offer. When they feel sorry for themselves because they feel nobody understands, I remind them that there was a time when I was in the same situation. This helps them to realize that I understand, and it breaks down the barriers they may have built up (against me or other members of the staff) that say, "No one understands what I'm going through."

In sharing myself with them, they learn to know that I understand, and that there is hope for them. If *I* can make it, that is, do something with my life with God's help, they can too. All they need is a desire to allow God and others to help them, and then also be willing to help themselves.

I have something special to give to the person who feels that no one cares. I have felt that way, too. I have felt alone, unloved, and as though there were no solution to my problems. Through my illness I have experienced a part of life that has enabled me to serve others in a special way. God has become meaningful in a way that I had never known before. I began to see his love and acceptance. My experience face to face with death has freed me to be open with God so that I can be of service to him in a very special way. I am even confident enough to believe that I was led into the chaplaincy so that I could be of help to those who have to walk the same path that I have walked.

Just as I am able to see my illness as an experience for more intimate, meaningful service, so do others. The following is an account of a very special young adult who used his illness as an opportunity for service.

Illness Is a Time for Service

I had known Roger more than five years, an intelligent, aggressive, handsome boy. He was the product of a broken marriage, a mother who was chemically dependent, a father who was immature, and a stepfather who was also chemically dependent.

Then it was discovered that he had leukemia. This was a terrible blow to him and to his family. He had life ahead of him. Why should this happen to him? Hadn't he had enough?

During the first few months of his illness, these questions plagued Roger. Even though he had committed his life to Christ at a retreat, he found himself angry and afraid. He usually took out his anger and fear on his mother and his younger brother. During the first nine months of his illness, he and his younger brother grew to resent each other more and more, and his mother had become so distraught over the whole situation that she was close to breaking under the pressure.

I remember the session I had with Roger, his mother, stepfather, and brother. I confronted Roger with the way he was abusing his family and using his illness to excuse his inappropriate behavior. It was hard for me to do this because I knew how sick he was. I also knew that unless he changed, he would isolate himself from his family and even perhaps from God. He would be alone in his dying, and the hardest thing about dying is not the act of dying but having no one, neither God nor people, supportively present. I knew he needed help in facing his dying, as all of us will, whether our faith is great or not.

Shortly after our meeting, Roger had to go back to the hospital. His blood had become so low that he needed more transfusions. This was very hard for him to accept. I am sure though that his return to the hospital helped him to be more realistic about his condition.

During the last two months in the hospital Roger's attitude began to change. He was no longer taking his anger out on his family, wallowing in self-pity, or being overwhelmed by his fears. He had accepted his dying. The only thing upsetting to him was that he had to go back on drugs to kill the pain. When he discovered this, he told his doctor, "You know, Doctor, it's really okay for me to die; and if it's okay with me, why isn't it okay with you?" He told his doctor that he and the Lord had it all worked out.

But he didn't stop there. He began to challenge them about their faith, as well as the nurses, housekeepers, visitors, patients, and even his own family. He knew that his time was short and he wanted to share the joy that he had found in Christ.

When Roger became sick he had three wishes he hoped would be fulfilled: to have the courage to face his own death; to have his mother, who is a recovering alcoholic, grow in her relationship with Christ; and to have his father accept Jesus Christ as his personal Savior. All of these wishes came true, and many more, because he used his illness as an opportunity for service to God and others.

He spent a great deal of time with other patients. He made visits to see the girl in the kidney unit. He wanted to do everything he could to encourage her. He also befriended a boy who was hydrocephalic. Often he had admired Roger's cap. Roger also found out that he liked the color blue. So one day he asked his mother to buy him a blue cap. Oh, to have seen the joy on that boy's face!

There was the little boy in the next bed who loved "Jingle Bells," and Roger would play it for him on his harmonica. And there was the boy from Chile who was to have open heart surgery. Roger used to chat with him from time to time. One day he asked Roger about death. Roger told him that he knew he would be dying soon. Roger assured him that death was okay and there was nothing to fear because he would be with God. I am sure that those words were a special comfort to that little boy from Chile because he died during surgery.

Shortly before Roger died, he made a special effort

to go to church with his mother and stepfather on
Mother's Day. His pain was very severe. It was so
bad that he cried through most of the service. But
he wanted to be there because he knew what this
would mean for his mother. He also visited his father
one weekend under the pretense that he wanted to
see how his father was coming with the boat he was
building. With the pain as severe as it was, it is not
too difficult to discern that he did it mostly to please
his father.

His devotional life was a service to others too.
He had disciplined himself to spend time reading,
praying, talking to others, and resting. Toward the
end, his sight had become so bad that his family and
others had to read for him. He followed his prayer
list faithfully every day. And his favorite books of
comfort and strength were: "What Is Heaven Like?"
"Lord of the Valley," and "To Die Is Gain." From
these books he had gleaned several gems of wisdom
which he would share whenever there was an opportunity. One of them was, "God said it, I believe it,
and that settles it for me!"

One of the most moving experiences was his reconciliation with his brother. They had been at odds
with each other most of their lives, but during
Roger's illness the gap had become wider. Even
though this was true, his brother continued to come
to see him. One day Roger insisted on speaking to
his brother alone. Roger told him how sorry he was
for treating him the way he had. They talked of
Roger's dying, how this was okay with Roger and
how he hoped that it was okay with his brother.
Their conversation was interrupted by their mother

walking in to find them hugging each other, crying and laughing all at the same time. This reconciliation came two days before he died.

The hardest time for Roger was at night when he was alone. Then he couldn't read, and his insecurities seemed to be more apparent. He found strength in praying for the assurance of Christ's presence. His days, however, were filled with caring, sharing, and serving.

Death came for Roger in the spring of the year. The night before he died his mother sensed that the next day would be the end. For some reason, though, she felt good about going home that night. She had the assurance that there was no unfinished business between herself and her son and that dying was okay with him. She had left him with a nurse who had come back on her time off and had agreed to be with him that night. She spent most of the night reading to him from Scripture, and in prayer and sharing.

Strangely, his mother slept better that night than she had for months. Something was telling her that she would need her rest for the next day and the days that followed. They would be difficult. Even though Roger had assured her that "it was okay with him," it would be hard to give him up. She had grown so close to him in these last months. Not only had she grown closer to Roger, but she had grown closer to God through Roger. She had even learned to accept her ex-husband's wife. This had happened one day when Roger had asked her to pray with her ex-husband and his wife. Roger had brought the three of them together with him. It would have been difficult for her to have any ill feeling toward someone who had cared about Roger. Maybe she hadn't cared as much as Roger's mother, but she had grown to love him, too.

Roger's mother arrived early that morning as usual. The pain had become worse. They were trying to relieve it with morphine in spite of Roger's protests. He didn't want to be in a stupor so that he wouldn't be able to share those precious moments with his family.

They spent the day quietly. There were times of reading, praying, and sharing. The cancer had progressed so far that Roger was only seeing shadows and his legs were paralyzed. His abcess had grown larger, his cheeks were puffed, and his hair was gone. Yet, he didn't seem to be ashamed of how he looked. He was always happy and willing to tell others about what he had found in the Lord.

At 4:00 p.m. he was given his last shot of morphine. He went to sleep and never awakened. He died about two hours later.

Almost automatically his mother stood up from her chair beside his bed and turned off the intravenous feeding. The end had come and there was beauty in his dying. It was as if she were saying by her actions, "I don't want anything here on earth to hold him back from going to be with God—not even the tube for intravenous feeding."

She walked to the window. As she looked through the window, she could see a lone bird begin to fly upward. It went higher and higher until it was out of sight. A sense of relief came over her. It was as if that lone bird were her son. Roger had gone to be with God. Tears ran down her cheeks, not tears of sorrow, but tears of thanksgiving.

As she was leaving the hospital she was met by a friend of Roger's whom the hospital had notified. He was carrying a bouquet of a dozen yellow roses. "These are for you," he said. "Roger told me to give them to you when he died. He wanted you to know how much he loved you. These are to say, Good-bye!"

Illness for Roger was an encounter with life, a part of life he had never experienced before. It wasn't something to be avoided. It was a time to care, to love, to share, and to serve. It was a time to glorify Christ, "whether by life or by death."

Roger's illness became a means to help others to see the value of illness. He had helped them see that it was a time for joy, reconciliation, and love. It was a time of opportunity, maturity, growth, and service. It had been the most meaningful time in his sixteen years of living.

By serving others, Roger had made his illness count.

Lord, growing up is hard work.
If only it could be easier.
If only I could avoid the hurts,
    disappointments, and dead ends.

Unfortunately, Lord, you know how hard it is
    for us to see what it is that makes life joyful.
We learn so hard.
We accept our fallibility so slowly.
Forgive us.

But sometimes it is through the difficulties of life
    that we discover the real values in living.
Illness is sometimes that special part of unexperienced
    life that helps us to see the values that last.
That loving, sharing, and serving God and others
    are the things that follow us into eternity
    and set us apart as "adult" in a world of children.

Lord, you know that it is only when we have grown up,
    when we have become secure in our faith
    because there is nothing else that lasts,
    that we are willing to be open to you—
    to surrender.
To be led by you without our knowing
    where you are going to be leading us.
"For to me to live is Christ, and to die is gain."

Lord, grant us the faith to risk serving you
    and the hope to perceive its value.

Amen

A Final Word

For many people illness has become the opportunity they have needed to mature as individuals, to grow in wisdom, and to serve others. Through illness they have found a meaning to life that they had missed. In illness many have discovered a way to tap the emotional strengths and spiritual powers available to every person who is a child of God.

Some time ago I heard the old story of the poor little girl who spent a day with the family of a rich aunt. This family had maids, butlers, and other servants who did everything for them. In fact, her aunt's family became very sheltered and dependent because everything was done for them.

That evening when the little girl went home she appeared disturbed. Finally, her mother asked her what was bothering her. "Mom," she said, "how can they ever learn? They never have to do anything."

Some of us may learn and mature only by doing unpleasant things or enduring unpleasant experiences. People everywhere of every religious persuasion have found illness to be one of the most meaningful and productive experiences of their lives. You can, too!

You can make your illness count, if you are willing to see your illness as an opportunity for God's healing power to be released in your life. Then, through the experience of denial being overcome by hope, anger by forgiveness, guilt by confession, fear by love, and manipulation by repentance—you will encounter the joy of maturity, wisdom, and service.

May God help us all to be open channels for his healing power—physically, emotionally, and spiritually.